Renovating the Heart

Inviting God to Cleanse, Renew, and Redeem Every Room of Your Spiritual House

Natalie Smith-Wells

Bean Tree Press

Copyright © 2026 by Natalie Smith-Wells.

All rights reserved.

10 9 8 7 6 5 4 3 2 1

Layout and Cover Design by Bean Tree Press
ISBN: 979-8-9944421-0-4
Printed in the United States of America.

Unless otherwise indicated, all Scripture quotations are taken from the Holy Bible, New Living Translation, copyright © 1996, 2004, 2015 by Tyndale House Foundation. Used by permission of Tyndale House Publishers, Carol Stream, Illinois 60188. All rights reserved.

No portion of this book may be reproduced in any form without written permission from the publisher or author, except as permitted by U.S. copyright law.

Contents

Dedication	1
Foreword	3
Author's Note	7
Why You Need to Renovate the Heart	9
Living Room	13
Kitchen	37
Kid's Room	55
Single Bedroom	77
Married Bedroom	95
Bathroom	109
Office	125
Closet	143
Basement	157
The Heart	173
About the Author	179

This book is dedicated to my late Aunt Willie.

You embodied love and compassion in the purest form. You would literally give the clothes off your back to anyone in need (oh the stories I could tell), and your infectious laugh had a way of lighting up even the darkest of days. Drawn to the underdog and the outcast, you made everyone feel like they were your favorite, with a love that was palpable and infectious.

Your sense of style and class were unmatched, and there wasn't a jealous or envious bone in your body. You celebrated everyone from a place of genuine sincerity, loving with intention and without expecting anything in return. Your presence is missed and cherished every day of my life. I'm deeply grateful to my mother for allowing me the opportunity to be loved by her big sister, a woman who made an indelible mark on my heart and the hearts of everyone who knew you.

Love forever and always,
Natalie

Foreword

Two Messages of Hope

The Bible is rich in metaphor, and one of its most compelling images is that of a house. Jesus used this image often—warning of the danger of leaving a cleansed house empty, and concluding His Sermon on the Mount with the well-known parable of the wise and foolish builders. Natalie Smith-Wells borrows this biblical language beautifully in this book, inviting readers to examine, remodel, and renovate their spiritual house.

I have known Natalie for more than twenty-five years—first as a nineteen-year-old college student, then as a coach traveling across the South, and now as the wife, friend, and woman of faith she is today. Over the decades, I have watched her face challenges, learn difficult lessons, and emerge with humility and grace. What she writes here is not mere theory—it is lived experience. That honesty is one of the qualities that makes this book so valuable.

Although this work is written primarily for women, it caused me to reflect deeply on my own life as a man. The chapters on the living room, bedroom, and closet especially resonated with me. I grew up in a family that kept secrets—a home where vulnerability was neither taught nor allowed. Those patterns of secrecy and fear of openness followed me into adulthood, affected my marriage, and even hindered my relationship with my Heavenly Father. Reading Natalie's candid stories helped me realize that the hidden places of the heart require thoughtful, patient, and diligent work.

Several years ago, I renovated my childhood home, which was built in 1950. Like many who have taken on such a project, I quickly discovered that renovation is costly. I also learned that it must be done one room at a time. I wanted everything finished quickly, but because I was serving as my own contractor—and working within a budget—I had to take my time. I came to understand that good renovation requires patience and care. As I read this book, I was reminded of that process. Spiritual renovation, like physical renovation, demands honesty, courage, and perseverance. The house I grew up in didn't deteriorate overnight, and neither would I be restored overnight. "Rome wasn't built in a day," and neither is the human soul. True renovation takes time, and shortcuts only weaken the foundation.

Renovation is an ongoing process. As a homeowner, I know that kitchens, living rooms, and systems must be repaired and updated over the years. So too is the inner life—our spiritual house must be revisited and renewed continually. Natalie's approach is practical and timeless, relevant to readers of every background, class, culture, and gender. Applying the principles she lays out in this book will bring healing, hope, and lasting transformation to anyone willing to do the work.

I encourage you to read this book contemplatively and prayerfully. Share what you learn with a friend or spiritual mentor, and commit to journaling your reflections along the way. When you do, God will work—and your life will be transformed.

—Dr. Timothy R. Fuller, Ph.D.

There are books you read, and there are books that read you. *Renovating the Heart* is one of the latter. As I turned each page, I could feel God inviting me, not into someone else's story, but into my own rooms: the ones I have decorated with faith, the ones I have neglected out of fear, and the ones I have kept locked because they hurt too much to enter. The chapter that stopped me in my tracks was "The Battlefield of the Bedroom." It reminded me that even in the spaces we've declared off-limits, where the lights are dim and the air feels heavy with regret or weariness, God still walks in. The good news is this: "He enters rooms we've locked. He redeems places we've abandoned. He heals what's happened in the dark."

Natalie Smith-Wells writes with the courage of a woman who has walked through her own renovation and lived to testify about the beauty on the other side. Her words are equal parts confession and invitation, calling us to examine the blueprints of our hearts and to trust the Master Builder with the repairs we cannot make alone. What I love most about her writing is

how practical and poetic it is at the same time, rich in Scripture, full of lived wisdom, and anchored in the kind of faith that has seen both storms and sunrises.

Reading this book feels like sitting in a quiet room with a trusted friend who tells you the truth, but tells it with love. Natalie doesn't rush the reader to wholeness; she walks beside you as you sift through the clutter, sweep away the shame, and make space for grace to move in. If you've ever felt stuck in a season of spiritual disarray, if you've wondered whether God could use what's been broken in you, this book will remind you that He not only can, but He delights in doing so. Every chapter is a room of revelation, and by the time you reach the end, you will have witnessed what redemption really looks like: not perfection, but presence.

So, open the door. Step into this house of healing. Let these pages guide you through the renovation you didn't even know you were ready for. The Carpenter has been waiting.

—Dr. Seneka R. Gainer

Author's Note

In May 2010, while I was serving as a collegiate coach at Georgia Southern University and an assistant pastor at Spirit and Truth Worship Center in Statesboro, GA, a transformative idea took shape. This concept was born from my observations of how we often invest time and energy in external renovations, whether it's improving our homes or perfecting our appearances—while neglecting the most crucial renovation of all: the renovation of our inner selves.

During that time, I proposed a Sunday School Series to my Pastor centered on the blueprint of a home and eight rooms typical to most houses. Each room serves as a framework through which to explore the relationship between our lives and our spiritual wellbeing. Just as a physical house requires maintenance and upgrades, so too does our spiritual house—the place where the soul, mind, will and emotions reside.

To bring this vision to life, I recruited three of my ministerial colleagues to walk with me in this teaching series. Together, we aimed to provide practical wisdom and spiritual guidance, helping individuals understand the importance of self-reflection and the continuous process of self-renovation. Each room in the house was not just a physical space but a metaphorical representation of different aspects of our lives.

Several friends also encouraged me over the years to write the book, including Nicole Brown and Ashley Hart, the latter of whom has been cheering me on since 2009.

The Word of God played a pivotal role in this journey. It served as the blueprint for every session, providing wisdom, direction, and insight, helping us to see ourselves through God's eyes and understand the divine purpose for our lives. This divine guidance was essential in helping us navigate the rooms of our spiritual house, revealing the areas that needed renovation and the steps necessary for growth and transformation.

Fifteen years later, this concept remains as relevant and vital as ever. In our fast-paced, constantly changing world, the need for deep, personal reflection and spiritual renewal is more crucial than ever. Our everyday lives are filled with distractions and challenges that can easily lead us away from our true selves, which can only be found in a thriving relationship with God through His son Jesus and His Word. The exploration of our spiritual house provides a path to understanding and valuing our inner essence. Each room offers insights that can guide us towards a more fulfilling and purposeful life.

While all houses may not have these eight specific rooms—and some houses may have many more such rooms—I pray this journey through the "rooms" of our lives will bring you closer to the incredible peace of knowing Christ our Lord.

As He promises us in John 14:2, "In my Father's house are many rooms. If it were not so, would I have told you that I go to prepare a place for you?"

May your "house" always grow closer and closer to the love, joy, and tranquility of that Heavenly House which has been promised us.

Why You Need to Renovate the Heart

In July 2005, a captivating show called *Flip This House* debuted on the A&E network. Shining a spotlight on the exciting world of real estate renovation, each episode showcased the thrilling journey of purchasing, renovating, and transforming a single property, complete with the costs, potential profits, and market values.

As the years have passed, this genre has become a television sensation, flooding our screens with home improvement shows like *Flip or Flop*, *Property Brothers*, and my personal favorite, *Fixer Upper*.

But here's the irony: We can spend hours engrossed in these makeover marathons without sparing a moment for self-reflection and personal growth concerning the house that we live in.

I'll confess—there's nothing I enjoy more than curling up on the couch with a freshly warmed blanket, a steaming cup of tea, and some delicious chocolate, indulging in endless episodes of home renovation shows. But it struck me—while we walk through our physical houses every day, we rarely invest time in the most important house of all, which is **the spiritual house**, the one that holds the soul, mind, will, and emotions. It's sad but true.

We spend hours consuming entertainment about homes we'll never see or live in, yet we forget that our lifelong home—the spirit—requires constant care and investment.

How recently have you considered the state of your bodily home? The clutter? Wear and tear? Perhaps even a spot that's given way to rot or an infestation?

It's tremendous fun to watch designers, buyers, and sellers haggle over purchase prices, renovation budgets, and market values, but nothing is more important than devoting ourselves to the betterment of our spiritual homes.

I can rattle off facts about Chip and Joanna Gaines or Jonathan and Drew Scott with ease. Many of us can!

But ask yourself: When was the last time you took a good look at the rooms of your inner house? When was the last time you took stock of its condition?

If it's been a while, don't feel ashamed. You are not alone. Every day, I meet people who have little awareness of their intrinsic value, or what it would take to enhance even one room in their internal house.

I firmly believe that every person walking on this earth has immeasurable worth that far exceeds any material possession or visible asset. Your spiritual house is a major part of that.

Clothed by our natural bodies, we are of greater value than any brick-and-mortar home for several reasons.

First, your body is the sanctuary where your true essence—your thoughts, emotions, and spirit—resides. It is the core of your being, influencing how you interact with the world and shape your experiences.

Second, unlike physical structures that can deteriorate over time, your spiritual house has the potential for continuous growth, renewal, and transformation. Investing in it yields profound, lasting benefits that go beyond mere appearances.

Lastly, while a physical house may offer shelter and comfort, it is your inner house that provides true fulfillment, peace, and purpose, guiding you through life's journey with resilience and grace.

This journey of self-exploration is vital because within each room of the spiritual house lie clues that reveal why we are the way we are.

Each "room" holds a key to understanding our deepest fears, our strongest desires, and our most cherished dreams. By examining and renovating these spaces, we not only uncover hidden truths but also unlock our potential to become the best versions of ourselves.

The Word of God is an essential guide in this journey. It provides wisdom, direction, and insight, helping us to see ourselves through God's eyes and understand the divine purpose for our lives.

It is my prayer that this journey will guide you through a thorough renovation of your spiritual house; that any clutter and rot will be found out and removed.

That all discouragement and damage—the remnants of regret, fear, shame, and guilt—will be demolished and cast out of your house forever.

That your heart can enjoy a beautiful, complete renovation.

That the before-and-after pictures will bring tears to your eyes, not because they're bought with money or adorned with the latest styles, but because they represent the greatest investment in your spirit you've ever made.

Let's begin the journey together.

Let's start the renovation.

Living Room

The Room of Speech and Silence

"Death and life are in the power of the tongue, and those who love it will eat its fruits." —Proverbs 18:21

Everything changed the day my grandmother stuck her foot in her purse as if it was her shoe.

Mama was sitting in her chair in the living room just as she did everyday. It was time to go to Winns, a treasure trove store much like today's Dollar General.

"Natalie, bring me my shoes," she called.

"Yes, Mama," I answered.

Nine years old, I adored my grandmother. She'd already raised twelve children and gladly took me in as her thirteenth. However, I was two decades younger than her own offspring and she was getting quite advanced in years.

I entered the living room and found her where I expected her to be: In her chair beside the screen door. She liked sitting there so she could see what was going on outside.

I glanced about the room to find her shoes and quickly spotted them. The pair lay on the floor right beside her, resting against her purse.

However, Mama stared at me with a frown.

"Where are my shoes?" she said, clearly unhappy.

My eyes glanced at the footwear close by but I didn't say anything. One didn't talk back to Mama. She'd raised a dozen kids before me, and her words carried the weight of that authority. There was nothing I could get past her.

Simply put: Mama did not play!

Even so, her unwavering support and care provided a stable foundation during my early years, creating a sense of safety and belonging as the two of us constantly spent time in the living room together.

Given that, I figured she meant a different pair of shoes. I dutifully turned and hurried to her room and brought back the only other pair of daily shoes I knew she wore.

Yet when I returned, I gasped. Mama was shoving her foot into her purse!

I laughed, thinking it was a rare moment of humor from her.

But my laughter quickly turned to concern as I realized something wasn't right. Her eyes narrowed at the small bag and she made quiet, frustrating grunts with the effort.

"Mama, what are you doing?"

She turned to me with a sharp scowl, then hastily took her foot out.

"Did you want these?" I said, holding up the second pair.

"No," she said, shaking her head. "My *shoes,* Natalie. Get my shoes."

Something was wrong. I couldn't describe it—I was nine years old, so how could I?—but I felt it in every part of my body.

I returned to her room and scoured the floor and closet for any other shoes she might be referring to, but found nothing.

Would she scold me for not finding the right pair? What was the deal with the purse?

I felt terribly confused, and at the same time terribly guilty of some indescribable crime.

Holding my breath, I made my way back to the living room.

Her foot was back in the purse.

As if to be funny, her other foot had somehow made its way into a shoe. But it was the other, jammed into her purse, that made me feel a sickness in my gut.

I knelt on the floor by her chair and said, "Let me help you, Mama."

With the most tender hands possible, I removed her foot from the purse and put the proper shoe on.

Suddenly she shook, as if from an icy chill, and snapped back to reality.

"What are you doing?" she cried. "Let go of my foot!"

I swallowed, the nausea twisting in my guts. "Just a minute, Mama," I whispered.

I slipped her shoe on the other foot, backed away, and sat with my head down.

It was time to go to Winns.

But at that moment, I didn't want to go anywhere except my room so I could curl up on my bed and figure out what the heck was wrong with Mama.

The Living, Not the Dead

Growing up, my maternal grandmother's living room was a place of warmth and familiarity. This is how it is supposed to be.

The Living Room may be an informal, all-purpose room, designed as a place where family and guests gather for activities like talking, reading, watching TV, and other forms of recreation.

However, I've found it is much more than that.

The Living Room is the place where we talk about our lives and the people living in them.

Ironically, the "living room" wasn't always known by this term. Before the end of the nineteenth century, this space was referred to as the "Death Room." This stemmed from its primary use during that period as a space for wakes and funeral services, which were often held at home. This space served as the proper place for viewing deceased family members. It was also a common practice for families to take post-mortem photographs in this room, preserving the last images of their loved ones.

As medical care improved over the years, and mortality rates decreased, the grim association of this room with death began to subside. In 1910, the *Ladies Home Journal* proposed that this room, no longer primarily a space of mourning, should be renamed to reflect its new, more positive role in the household. The magazine suggested calling it the "Living Room" to emphasize life and family gatherings.

This change transformed the space into a welcoming area for relaxation, entertainment, and socialization, and it became known simply as the "parlor" or "living room." And since it is such a central space—common, shared, and designed to meet the needs of everyone in the house—it is frequently the space where stories are told.

This was absolutely true of my grandmother's house. She regularly held court in her living room, telling stories and giving wise lessons to her children, and to me. Mama Smith, the matriarch of the family, was a woman of wisdom who knew how to create a home that was stable and safe.

Yet beneath this hospitable exterior, many unspoken questions were left to fester. Sure, I felt safe there; but I also felt the weight of things left unsaid.

That Saturday morning, as my grandmother did her best Cinderellea impression with that purse, something changed in me. I realized that fundamental elements of my childhood—and therefore the identity I had been forming—had been broken the whole time without me knowing it.

To this day, that morning haunts me; I have no doubt there are similar moments from your life that still live with you, deeply saddening and fearful moments.

The human heart is not made for secrets. Yes, we commit these sins due to our fall from God's grace, but doing so is unnatural and we know it. If it wasn't, then we'd feel no shame or need to defend ourselves.

My family isn't unique in this regard. I don't blame anyone in my family in particular. However, just because faulty communication is common doesn't mean it is good or wise.

While lies, misdirections, and cover-ups can happen in any room of the house, there is one room where they happen the most: The Living Room.

Threats to the Living

Despite its rebranding in the early 1900s, the Living Room is starting to revert back to its old name and role.

It has become rare to see families spending quality time in the living room, except during special occasions like holidays and birthdays. This shift has led to a decline in communication within the household. With everyone absorbed in their own devices, phones, laptops, games—we have shut the door on meaningful interactions with those living under the same roof. It's not uncommon to look around a room of people and see everyone looking at a screen. We are like moths drawn to the light of distraction and entertainment, neglecting to give our best presence to the human beings around us.

Not to say that families never communicate. Some still hold important "family meetings" when serious or pressing matters arise. Some set aside time for family activities, like board or card games, conversations, or devotionals.

But this is becoming rarer by the day.

Sure, we may no longer lay our deceased loved ones out for display, but our relationships are dying.

Imagine not needing to call a family meeting because our daily communication and time spent together in the living room were filled with healthy, intentional interactions. The living room, once the heart of the home, could reclaim its role as a space for connection and communication, enriching our family lives and strengthening our bonds.

If we neglect to communicate with one another, it poisons our relationships. Worse, when we fail to honor the truth with our words—or by withholding those words—we plant seeds of trauma that will inevitably blossom into terrible damage in the future of our families.

This was true for me.

While Mama's house was comfortable and safe, it wasn't always honest, *especially* when it came to the matter of my parents.

My Secret

All throughout my youth, silent mysteries loomed over me. I had so many unanswered questions growing up: Why was I living with her instead of my parents? Why did I only see my mother once in a while?

Why was my skin so much lighter than the rest of my family? And where was my father?

My Aunt Willie was a gift from the Lord and played a significant role in raising me in my formative years. She took me shopping with her and always treated me to a meal out, introducing me to the cuisine of Dairy Queen (I still like a good Butterfinger Blizzard), the local Mexican joint, Jim's Krispy Fried Chicken, and even Luby's if we went out of town.

These outings were a welcome contrast to the traditional Southern meals at home, enriching my culinary experiences and making me appreciate the diversity. They also added a layer of joy and variety to my childhood and created cherished memories that complemented the loving, yet routine, atmosphere at home.

Yet somehow their presence accented the fact that I *wasn't* enjoying these moments with the man and woman who brought me into the world.

Why not?

No one talked about it. No one mentioned my father, and no one—truly, *nobody*—ever said anything about the relative lightness of my skin compared to Mama and Aunt Willie.

Like any dutiful child, I took the silence as a sign to let it be. If the grown folks didn't bring it up, I shouldn't either. But that didn't stop me from wondering, night after night, what was being hidden from me, and why.

Even more troubling, I began noticing more changes in my grandmother. The purse moment had been startling, but I tried to explain it away in my mind.

Mama's being funny, I thought. *But Mama is never silly like that. What in the world is going on?*

This wasn't the only contradiction to leave me isolated and confused. It was as if I'd been left to wonder if it was all in my head. The silence weighed more heavily than a mountain and I always felt crushed by its palpable bulk, as if speaking the truth might cause it to crash down and crush me completely.

These unspoken questions created a sense of isolation and confusion, leaving me to navigate my identity and family dynamics without guidance or understanding.

As the days went on, the silence in our metaphoric living room became more pronounced, until it broke open.

And just as I feared, I was the one caught in the collapse.

Driving Mama

Mama was losing weight.

A lot of it.

In fact, I quickly noticed she would wear two outfits at the same time so others would not notice. There were also times I saw red stains on her clothing—it had to be blood, right?—which she would hastily hide in a backroom closet. She never did her wash when I was home, either, but always while I was at school.

These were alarming signs; still, no one said a thing about them.

This silence profoundly impacted my life, unknowingly shaping my perceptions of family, trust, and the importance of open dialogue.

It felt as though the living room, a space meant for connection and conversation, had become a place of secrets and unspoken fears.

That same day—the Saturday when Mama had tried to wear her purse as a shoe—she and I loaded up in her brown 1980s Chevrolet to run to Winns.

As we left the store and walked to the parked car, Mama did something I didn't expect: Instead of heading to the driver's seat, she veered towards the passenger door alongside me. With a stern look that could cut through steel, she yelled, "Girl, where are you going? Hurry up and get in the car and get us out of here!"

I was bewildered. At just nine years old, the idea that she expected me to drive was unfathomable. Yet fear and respect forced me to the driver's side, and I opened the door and slipped in behind the wheel. It was enormous. I could barely see over the dashboard.

Am I really about to do this? I wondered in panic.

I couldn't drive. Physically, legally—it was impossible!

But Mama's word was law, and I knew better than to disobey her, especially with her "heavy hand."

So for a good thirty seconds we sat beside one another on that old Chevy bench seat. We buckled our seatbelts, and she handed me the keys. I reached for the gearshift. I'd seen her drive a thousand times and I figured, *This is how you start.* My heart pounded. I stuck my foot out, wiggling my toes to find the brake pedal.

Then, as if jolted back to reality, Mama snapped, "Girl, what do you think you are doing?" Her eyes were wide and round with panic filled her eyes, and her hand flew to the wheel to hold it in place.

Voice trembling, I whimpered, "I'm about to drive us home."

Quickly, she unbuckled her seatbelt, rushed around the car, and reclaimed her position as the driver. She unhooked my seatbelt and pushed me across the bench with a mix of panic and frustration. I couldn't understand why she was upset with me, considering she had forced me to take the wheel.

I wanted to ask questions. I wanted to know why the heck I'd nearly driven an automobile before the age of ten. I wanted to know I was still safe.

But fear kept me quiet. A culture of silence had made it clear: Whatever the truth was, I wasn't supposed to know it.

You Told on Me

Just because I was young didn't mean I was the only one that Mama was keeping secrets from.

The following Wednesday, my aunt picked me up from school on her day off to take me to Dairy Queen.

It took less than 5 minutes for the dam to break.

I tried to stay silent. That's what I'd been taught to do!

But I must have been trembling or visibly fighting back tears, so Aunt Willie asked, "What's wrong, Natalie?"

Tears welled up in my eyes and I confessed, "There's something wrong with Mama."

I spilled everything—the purse incident, double clothing, the blood-stained shirts, and the driving mishap. I saw my aunt's face fall.

Then, without a word, she quickly packed up our meals and hurried us to the car. We headed straight to the pharmacy behind Dairy Queen.

In a small town of 3,000, everyone knew everyone. My aunt asked directly for the pharmacist who greeted us warmly.

"I'm here to pick up my mom's prescriptions," she said.

His puzzled expression turned to concern as he reviewed my grandmother's file. "Willie, Mrs. Smith hasn't filled or picked up any of her medications in months."

My aunt gasped. With a knowing, defeated sigh, she shook her head and drove to my grandmother's house. Though the drive was less than a mile, it remains a fog in my memory. Guilt gnawed at me for "telling my grandmother's business."

However, that moment changed everything. It was the first time I realized the power of speaking the truth, even when it's uncomfortable. My words broke the silence, and in doing so, they opened the door for my aunt to get to the bottom of things.

At the house, as we sat in the living room, my aunt gently confronted her mother about the medications and the observations I had shared.

My grandmother gave me a look that still haunts me—a look that said, "You told on me."

Despite my guilt, I knew it was the right thing to do. My aunt sprang into action and made it her mission to get Mama back on track with her medication and begin restoring her health.

That haunting look, and the heavy silence that followed, revealed something deeper—how often we, as humans, choose to bear our struggles alone, shielding those we love from our pain.

Yet this is not how God designed us to walk in our struggles. God did not design us to hide our vulnerability from one another; rather, He made us to live in intimate community, allowing us to bear one another's burdens as much as possible.

Pride had robbed my family of that opportunity, and there's a good chance it's doing that to your family, too.

Pride: The Great Threat to Living

One doesn't think of keeping their pain or burdens to themselves as prideful. In our minds, it's an attempt to protect loved ones from hurt or worry.

Yet, this self-imposed silence creates a heavy burden, one that becomes even more profound when we realize it too late.

And despite our good intentions, it is indeed born of pride, a need to handle things ourselves and keep total control in our own hands.

Born in 1919, my grandmother was a product of her generation. Women of this time, especially Black women, were taught to endure in silence and shield their loved ones from their struggles.

But this lack of communication leads to heartache for those left in the dark, alone to grapple with questions and uncertainties.

When someone discovers a loved one's suffering, but only when it's too late to help, agonizing questions inevitably rise to the surface. I'm not sure of all the questions that flooded my aunt's mind over the next year, but these were some of the questions that many have at a time such as this:

- **Why didn't she (they) tell me?** A deep sense of confusion and betrayal might arise, wondering why the loved one chose to keep their suffering a secret.

- **How long has she (they) been carrying this pain?** There's often a need to understand the duration and extent of someone's struggle. Time multiplies trauma, and long-held secrets lead to exponential damage.

- **Did I miss the signs?** Guilt and self-doubt can lead to reflecting on past interactions and wondering if there were overlooked clues.

My aunt was certainly aware of my grandmother's previous diagnoses; however, she did not know the severity of the situation or my grandmother's decision to stop taking her medications. There's a huge difference between knowing there's a problem and knowing your loved one is doing nothing to manage that problem.

Other questions come to mind, unsolvable queries that haunt us and keep us lying sleepless through lonely nights:

- **Could I have done something if I knew earlier?** A lingering "what if" scenario, pondering whether earlier intervention could have made a difference.

- **Why did they feel the need to protect me?** Understanding a loved one's motives for keeping their pain hidden—often out of love and protection—can be complex.

- **How did they cope with their suffering alone?** Trying to imagine the loved one's inner world and how they managed their pain in solitude.

- **How do I navigate my own emotions about this?** Addressing personal feelings of sadness, guilt, and helplessness that arise from the revelation.

- **Can I forgive myself and my loved one?** Working through emotions to find a place of forgiveness for both oneself and the other, especially if they've passed away.

When we hoard our vulnerable challenges, we betray the very notion of what a family is and should be. We deny our loved ones the chance to sacrifice, to share, to invite others in, to empathize, and—most importantly—to pray. We tell ourselves, "I don't want to burden them," but the truth is that this prideful approach *is the burden.*

We have to talk to one another, and we must do so honestly. We must surrender our pride, put down the distractions, and open ourselves to the love of our closest companions.

We must be willing to renovate the space where we share our most vulnerable truths; that place is the Living Room, the space for connection.

Answers That Waited A Lifetime

It wasn't until the early hours of Saturday, April 17, 2021, at precisely 5:05 AM, that I learned the truth.

It came in the form of a notification, jolting me awake. I rolled over and read, *Your AncestryDNA results are in!*

Almost two years before this revelation, my friends Ashley, Abby, and Courtney had whisked me away on a cruise for my 40th birthday. I've always found it hard to be the center of attention, so their triumph in getting me to celebrate was an impressive win.

However, after the cruise, Ashley unexpectedly sent me an AncestryDNA kit. Unsure of her motive for sending it, I tucked the box away in the back of a closet. Of course, I knew deep down why she'd sent it—reaching your 40s often sparks a reckoning, a period of introspection where life's unanswered questions take center stage. During the cruise we'd shared countless stories of childhood and upbringing, and Ashley must have noticed that there was a haunting silence around the topic of my parentage.

Two years later, while cleaning out my closet, I reached up to reorganize my shoes only to have something fall and hit me on the head. I rubbed my forehead and stared down at the culprit: *The Box.*

It seemed almost poetic, as if God was nudging me forward and saying, "It's time."

For the rest of the night, it occupied my thoughts. By morning, I resolved to complete the swab and mail it off.

I wasn't expecting much. I barely knew anything about my father—I knew of a potential name, but it felt more like a nickname. Yet that harmless email was about to unravel a closely guarded secret, illuminating mysteries that had overshadowed my life for decades.

The questions that filled the living room of my youth had now become the front porch of my 40s, forcing me to confront what had been avoided for so long.

Who was my father?

Sitting up in bed, the sun still an hour from rising, I opened the email and read the report.

I gasped. "Oh my God," I murmured.

That potential name, a name I had shrugged off as a mere nickname, wasn't just real—it was *him*.

It matched perfectly, revealing without a doubt that the man in the report was my father.

There was no turning back. The truth stood stark and undeniable: We shared the same blood.

As they say, "the blood doesn't lie."

Shock washed over me. Was I more stunned by the fact that my potential father had actually been found, or that my DNA painted a vastly different picture of my heritage than I had imagined?

A list of ethnic origins appeared that I never expected to see: Ireland. Scotland. Germany.

This was the answer. In a way I'd always known, but wondering is much different than truly, factually *knowing*.

As one question was answered, countless new ones began to emerge:

Who was this man who shared my blood?

Did he know whether or not I existed?

Did I have unknown siblings?

Was he still alive, and if so, could I find him?

Would he *want* to be found?

I wanted answers. I wanted the truth. It was like the ancestry report was the first taste of a new candy, and I wanted to eat the whole bag.

My mind was made up, and I started taking steps to locate him. This man may not have cared to know more about me, but I was determined to know more about him.

Praying With a Stranger

On a Monday morning a month after getting the results, I received the first text message from him while driving to work.

I pulled into a parking lot. My hands were steady on the wheel, yet the tension beneath the surface was unmistakable. I took a moment to gather myself, unsure how I felt about even having this information, much less receiving the message waiting for me.

I drew in a deep breath and exhaled slowly, trying to maintain a semblance of control over the whirlwind of thoughts running through my mind. Finally, I opened my eyes and shifted my focus to the phone in my hand. The message was there—waiting to be read, hinting at the possibility of a connection that had long been missing.

It was simple. Polite.

That's a good start.

We texted back and forth. As his messages arrived, I quickly gathered that he wasn't just responding to my existence; he was trying to process it.

Thankfully, there was an undeniable undertone of faith in his words, a heart for the things of God that shone through even in the brief sentences we exchanged.

By the time we agreed to set up a phone call for Friday, I wasn't sure what to expect. Would we talk about his life? Would he ask about mine? Would the conversation feel forced, or would it flow naturally?

For the next few days, I carried the weight of those questions. Every time I thought about the upcoming call, I found myself hovering between curiosity and hesitation, unsure if I wanted answers or if I wanted to keep my expectations low.

And then Friday came.

I wasn't looking for a profound connection or instant relationship—just a conversation. Maybe clarity. Maybe closure. I didn't know what I was looking for, but I knew I had to follow through.

The call itself was... awkward.

Neither of us asked many questions. Instead, we offered up pieces of surface-level information, almost as though we didn't know how to venture any deeper. He opened the conversation with, "I guess I'll start by sharing my testimony with you."

I listened as he spoke about his life, about how his faith had shaped him. It was unexpected yet fitting, a glimpse into the spiritual thread running through his story. And while I appreciated his openness, the entire interaction felt stilted—two strangers walking on unfamiliar ground, unsure of what lay ahead.

His words carried the weight of guarded emotion, each sentence a careful step on the fragile bridge we were trying to build. For most of the call, it felt as though we were circling around the reality of the moment, hesitant to land on its implications.

I wasn't angry or hurt; I understood. This was new, startling, and—frankly—a lot to process for both of us.

By the end of the call, his emotions seemed to bubble to the surface, breaking through the stoic guard he had maintained. There was a heaviness in his final words, a mix of overwhelm and uncertainty. I suggested we end with prayer.

I started, and when I finished, he began to pray as well.

When I hung up, I couldn't shake the feeling that this conversation might very well be our last.

But something stayed with me—something undeniable.

I had seen a picture of him by this point that his cousin shared with me via email, and the resemblances were striking. It was like looking into a mirror that reflected not just physical features but fragments of a shared history I was only beginning to uncover.

I didn't know what the future held.

But I knew one thing: Whatever it would be, the future would be one where truth took a front seat. There would be no room for pride and its deceptive schemes.

Not anymore.

Speak Truth, Speak Life

There is something sacred about the Living Room in a home. It's where we gather, laugh, celebrate, and, in its purest form, connect. It is meant to be a space of transparency, a heart of the household where relationships deepen, and the day's burdens are shared.

But what happens when the Living Room falls silent? When its quiet walls protect secrets that remain unspoken for years, or even decades?

My grandmother's illness and the revelation of my father's identity, seemingly separate threads, are woven together by a common truth:

Silence cannot not stop the truth from finding its way into the light.

Whether through physical signs of declining health, or the results of a DNA test stuffed in a closet and forgotten, the things we attempt to bury have a way of surfacing—often when we are least prepared for them.

For years, the silence in the living room of my grandmother's home shaped me. Her strength, her steady presence, and the unwavering love she provided were anchors in my young life, but there were questions that sat heavily, unspoken, in that space. While I was too afraid to ask these questions, I couldn't force myself to forget them.

And sadly, the answers didn't come from conversations in that room. They came from moments of crisis that shattered the silence—Mama's declining health revealing itself in the stains she tried to hide; a foot in a purse; an underage driving violation; and a tumbling ancestry kit knocking me on the head.

In this house called life, we often treat communication like a fragile thing, avoiding difficult conversations for fear of causing pain or discomfort. We convince ourselves that silence is a form of protection, and that by keeping certain truths hidden we are shielding others—or even ourselves—from harm.

But silence is never as harmless as it seems.

My grandmother, a woman of immense strength and wisdom, chose to keep her declining health a secret. Perhaps she didn't want to burden us with worry, or perhaps she believed she could manage it alone. Yet, as her health failed, the very silence that once protected us became a source of confusion and hurt, leaving us to piece together the truth from the fragments she could no longer hide.

Similarly, the unanswered questions about my father remained a quiet weight on my heart, shaping my sense of identity in ways I didn't fully realize until the truth finally revealed itself.

These experiences taught me something profound: There are conversations that are long overdue, waiting to be had in the living rooms of our lives.

These aren't easy conversations—they are the ones that require vulnerability, honesty, and courage.

But they are necessary. Because without them, the silence we maintain can become a barrier that separates us, leaving the people we love to wrestle with the very questions we could help them answer.

The Living Room, both in a home and as a metaphor for the spaces in our relationships, was never meant to hold silence. Its purpose is connection—real, raw, imperfect connection and communication. It's a space where we are called to sit with each other, to speak and to listen, to offer understanding and seek forgiveness, and to uncover the truths that set us free.

I hope you choose to let the light into your Living Room, turning it back into a place of warmth and honesty instead of a vault for unspoken truths. When we do, I promise you'll find that what emerges—though it may come with challenges—is the very thing that strengthens the foundation of your house called life.

This lesson extends beyond the walls of any home, reminding me that the lines of communication we choose to open don't just shape our relationships—they also shape the spiritual house we build with Jesus.

A Call for the Living

Too often, the Living Room becomes a space of silence—an archive of what goes unsaid. And in much the same way, our spiritual house is not immune to this kind of silence.

Just as families can keep secrets or avoid difficult conversations in their homes, we often do the same with Jesus. We hold onto our struggles, questions, and pain, tucking them away in the hidden corners of our hearts. We convince ourselves that He doesn't need to know—or worse, that He doesn't want to. But nothing could be further from the truth.

The purpose of the spiritual house we dwell in with Him mirrors the purpose of that living room in a home: It's a space for open communication, transparency, and connection.

Jesus wants us to bring every question, every burden, and every joy to Him.

He doesn't ask us to have all the answers or to present ourselves as put-together; He simply asks us to come.

Think about how life might look if we stopped holding back, if we allowed Him access to every room of our spiritual house, even the ones we've kept locked for years. What healing could come if we spoke the words we've buried, if we shared the weight we've carried alone?

The silence in my grandmother's living room, as well as the decades-long mystery surrounding my father, taught me that unspoken truths have a way of surfacing, whether we're ready for them or not. But with Jesus, we don't have to wait for crises or revelations to bring those things into the light. He is always there, ready to listen, ready to provide clarity, and ready to carry the burdens we were never meant to hold alone.

We serve a Savior who specializes in open doors and open hearts. He desires a relationship built on honesty and trust, where the living room of our spiritual house isn't a place of secrets but a sanctuary for communion with Him.

The power of keeping those lines of communication open is life-changing. When we speak to Him, we find peace for our restless hearts. When we listen to Him, we discover answers we didn't know we needed. And when we allow Him into the hidden spaces of our lives, we find freedom and healing beyond measure.

The Bible reminds us to "Cast your cares on the Lord and he will sustain you; he will never let the righteous fall," (Psalm 55:22). The word "cast" here implies throwing, hurling, or flinging with force and intention—inviting us to deliberately hand over our burdens to the Lord.

These "cares" represent the burdens or responsibilities that weigh us down, and the act of casting them onto the Lord signifies trusting Him to support us in managing these weights.

God never closes the door of communication with His children. He stands ready to listen, to care, and to provide comfort. By sharing our struggles with Him, we can find the strength and support we need, knowing that we will not be left unstable or insecure.

The truth is we can never fully renovate the Living Room of our hearts on our own; we need the One who created man's mouth, the Savior who shared Himself with us as the Word, the God who spoke and all of creation came into being. Only He can truly redeem this room on our behalf.

But when we surrender to Him, He is glad to complete that sanctifying work in our lives!

So be reminded of this truth: The invitation to connect is always there. With Jesus, no conversation is overdue, no question unwelcome, and no burden too heavy for Him to bear.

Questions for Reflection

1. What role does the living room play in your home? Is it a place of connection, or a vault of silence?

2. What important conversations have been avoided in your family? What do you fear will happen if you break that silence?

3. What is one conversation you need to have with a loved one this week?

Journaling Prompt

How can you create a culture of open communication in your home? What steps can you take to ensure your living room becomes a space of life and truth?

My Prayer for You

Father,

Thank you for the room of conversation—you who made us to speak and to listen, to share and to be still. I lift up the person reading now: For every word they have withheld out of fear, for every truth they've swallowed in silence, for every echo of shame in the quiet corners of their heart.

Lord, come into this living room of their spirit. Bring Your voice where theirs has faltered. Unravel the silence that hides their pain. Give them courage to speak the truth that sets them free—about what happened, what they believe, what they long for. Where they have felt unheard, may they discover that You have always been listening. Where they have spoken words that wounded others or themselves, bring Your grace for restoration.

May this room become a place of healing dialogue—with You and with those You send into their lives. Let laughter, honesty, sorrow, confession, and hope all live here under Your roof. May they find that in this place truth meets love, and silence meets Spirit.

In Jesus' Name, Amen

KITCHEN

THE ROOM OF HEAT AND RISK

"To everything there is a season, and a time to every purpose under the heaven." —Ecclesiastes 3:1

For years, my identity was wrapped up in coaching college track and field.

It was all I knew. This primary skill set was the sole avenue I saw for my life.

But one day, I felt something strange. I call it a divine nudge.

Whatever it was, it was urging me to do something radical and unexpected: Step away from my career.

Was God losing His marbles? Or was I going insane?

Immediately, I resisted this idea. It filled me with dread, uncertainty, and complete fear about the unknown.

Yet I noticed something: It was *thrilling*.

Not only was it possible that I could set out on a new adventure, but it seemed the Lord Himself was trying to get me to do it.

At the same time, it was terrifying. What if I didn't find another fulfilling career path? What if I found myself in an unsustainable position?

What if, what if, *what if?*

I realized that my mind was made up: I would leave my career in coaching.

But I had no idea how things would turn out, and this filled me with terror.

Still, the urging of the Holy Spirit was irresistible, so I put in my two-weeks and began to pray without ceasing.

Defying Limits

When I handed my resignation letter to the Athletic Director, something changed inside of me. I was still nervous, but a veil was pulled back from my eyes.

Suddenly I wasn't locked into this one position. I wasn't even confined to the role of "coach" anymore. I could take any step I wanted.

Of course this didn't mean I *would* take any old step. There were plenty of foolish steps I could have taken, and an abundance of silly choices ahead.

But by stepping away from this career that I'd let define me for so many years, I realized how limiting it was to build my entire sense of purpose on this one role. These limitations provided a steady paycheck, benefits, community, fulfillment—but I had outgrown them.

I began to see the possibilities that lay outside these limits. Self-employment. Entrepreneurship. Real estate. I saw opportunity everywhere, but with it, risk. I'd begun to imagine myself flipping houses like Chip and Joanna Gaines, but I knew the reality would be much different than a television show.

Could I pull it off? If a house ended up in the red, would I be able to rally with the next one?

And in all of this, was I really listening to the voice of God as I weighed and measured my options?

Until this point, I had been the kind of person who thinks, "I should stay in my lane and not seek anything else." Moreso, I've believed God thinks this about me too, which is why it was so shocking when these ideas started coming to me.

With this in mind, we would be wise to consider how we view God's attitude about risks, and whether our view of the Cross is big enough to trust Him with our scary choices. And if you come from a home like mine, there's no room where the temperature is higher than the kitchen!

The Room of Risky Heat

I love the kitchen.

Delicious smells. Delectable tastes. Thrilling sounds, like the clanging of pans, foreshadowing meals and memories.

But if you spend any length of time in a kitchen—especially as one preparing the meals—it can lose some of its luster.

In reality, the kitchen is dangerous, both physically and relationally.

It presents obvious physical dangers, like sharp edges, hot surfaces, splashing grease, raw ingredients, and not-so-obvious relational risks, like offending a proud family chef or overhearing a tidbit of gossip you'll wish you could have avoided.

Preparing food is inherently risky. You have to choose ingredients, temperatures, and cooking times. You must master complex processes, depending on which meal or delicacy you're creating.

This is why we have countless cooking shows, putting home cooks from around the world to the test: Top Chef, Masterchef, Is It Cake?, The Great British Baking Show.

Yet most of us didn't grow up eating dishes worthy of five-star restaurants. You may have eaten bland, poorly seasoned portions that left you asking to go to McDonalds. Or maybe you received delicious plates of food, but felt required to follow strict rules and procedures in order to keep the chef—often Mama or Papa—happy.

The Kitchen is a place where risky choices can bring remarkable joy or crushing shame; it is the literal crucible of the house, and it serves as a powerful symbol for how well or poorly we tolerate risks and the opinions others might have about them.

The Evolution of the Kitchen

While today the kitchen may be the heart of the home, it wasn't always so.

For several hundred years, the kitchen was often a hidden, utilitarian space occupied by servants. For the poor and middle class, kitchens were kept separate from eating areas and other shared spaces. There was no such thing as an "open concept" more than one hundred years ago.

The word "kitchen" itself comes from Latin, "cucina," signifying a place of cooking and nourishment. It's also where we get our word "cuisine" for the fruit of a kitchen. Old English influences morphed the word into the consonant-heavy term we use today, *kitch-en*.

Now that cooking is more than a mere act of survival, or a task delegated to the servant class, it truly embodies the process of making careful calculations prior to making bold choices. This process beautifully parallels the way we navigate life's challenges. Just as meals require preparation, patience, and adaptability, so do our personal and spiritual journeys.

The kitchen has also evolved to share dual purposes; it's not purely for preparation, at least in most homes. In fact, some families eat directly in the kitchen provided there is ample space. Others will gather and help the cook prepare the victuals or set the table, creating a space for connection, conversation, and creativity.

The kitchen's transformation over time seems to perfectly encapsulate the transformation of society over the centuries, and now emphasizes the importance of communal experiences and the significance of preparation in achieving desired outcomes.

Amidst the sizzle of hot pans, the hum of ovens, and the whirr of air fryers, the kitchen has become a place where many ponder life's mysteries and try to make sense of it all. That's why there's something inherently metaphorical about the preparation, timing, and processes in the kitchen that mirrors the trials and errors of life. Following a recipe feels safer than improvising and taking risks. While taste is crucial, plating and presentation have also become essential.

Methods have evolved, as well. For some, "low and slow" was the key to a great meal. Numerous disciplines, especially Texas Barbecue, swear by it.

However, we now live in a fast-paced world where speed often takes precedence. We want meals that can be microwaved, pressure-cooked, or heated in a small toaster oven in a matter of minutes. Our ingredients are rarely fresh anymore, loaded with secret preservatives and chemicals no one can read or pronounce.

Let us slow down and pause a moment, considering how the way we work with food in the kitchen mirrors our struggle to take healthy risks on this journey of life.

Cooking Outside Your Comfort Zone

Though I'm not a *Top Chef*-level cook, I have learned valuable life principles from my kitchen experiences. Unfortunately, many of these experiences have led me to play it safe—not just in the kitchen but in other areas of my life as well. I have often hesitated to embrace the creative adventures with the potential to push me out of my comfort zone, preferring instead the familiarity of routine.

The kitchen teaches us an important yet paradoxical lesson: Following a recipe may ensure success, but it's the moments of experimentation and risk-taking that truly enrich our lives and often lead to unexpected joy.

Much like cooking, life requires a balance between preparation and spontaneity. Sometimes we cling to what is safe and predictable, afraid to deviate from the known ingredients of our lives.

But true growth can only happen when we dare to mix things up.

Consider some questions we might ask in the kitchen and how they explore the delicate balance of risk-and-reward, both in the realm of cooking and decision-making.

"Is the heat too high, or am I just not prepared for it?"
Could you truly be under too much pressure, or do you need to adapt and grow through this challenge?

"What ingredients am I missing?"
You may want to prepare a dish or make a particular choice, but lack the necessary ingredients. What tools, skills, or support do you still need in order to navigate this phase of your life?

"How do I handle the mess I've made?"
Everyone makes messes of things, both in the kitchen and out. How do you clean up your mistakes and either salvage the effort or start fresh?

"Who's helping me, versus who's just making a mess?"
Are you surrounding yourself with people who uplift and support you and your efforts? Or are the people around you merely introducing constant chaos into your work?

"Do I trust the process, even when I can't see the results yet?"
Are you willing to have faith in the work you're putting in, even when progress feels slow?

"Is this dish meant for me, or am I cooking for someone else's taste?"
Are you living authentically, or are you trying to meet someone else's expectations?

"What's been left on the back burner for too long?"
What have you been neglecting that needs your attention and care?

The answers to these questions shape the way we navigate not just the kitchen, but life itself. Growth often requires adjusting the temperature, adding missing ingredients, and having the patience to let things develop in their own time.

Just as every cook has their own style, every person's journey is unique. What one person may not like, another may love.

To fully thrive in the kitchen of life, we must embrace our individual paths and trust that even when things seem uncertain, the right combination of experiences will create something truly fulfilling.

Kitchen Clichés as Guiding Principles for Life

Want to start renovating your Kitchen right now? You probably know a few catch-phrases that can help.

These sayings focus on *actual* kitchens, of course, but you'd be surprised how easily they apply to the spirit.

Here's what I mean:

"Too Many Cooks Spoil the Broth"

Much like in a busy kitchen, the right balance of voices can lead to a savory outcome while too many can spoil the broth. This kitchen cliché offers a guiding principle for life: Avoid overcrowding the metaphorical kitchen of your mind with too many opinions.

Proverbs 11:14 reminds us, "Where no counsel is, the people fall: but in the multitude of counselors there is safety."

Having too many opinions can lead to confusion and hinder progress. In personal and professional settings, seeking counsel from a trusted few rather than an overwhelming number of voices leads to clarity and direction. It is certainly vital to trust your own inner voice, but it is also crucial to acknowledge the importance of having a few trusted advisors. Balancing this dynamic ensures that your life is enriched by wisdom without being overwhelmed by conflicting advice.

"A Watched Pot Never Boils"

Impatience can make time feel endless. Often, we fixate on the things we want most—relationships, career advancements, personal breakthroughs—without recognizing that growth and change take time. Learning to wait while staying productive in other areas allows us to prepare for opportunities as they arise.

Have you ever found yourself waiting on a specific thing—perhaps the pursuit of a romantic partner, a large purchase like a house or car, or starting a new career—and the hours and days dragged by at a snail's pace? This phenomenon is universal.

Everyone has lost themselves in a "watched pot" at one time or another, and practically everyone finds themselves feeling the same thing as they wait: Emptiness.

Take the example of waiting for a job offer—refreshing your email inbox every few minutes only heightens the anxiety. You check it at 9:02, thinking that maybe the hiring manager is going to send out an offer first thing in the morning.

Nothing happens.

You try to distract yourself with some busywork. Then you check again.

No email.

The time?

9:07.

How has it only been five minutes!?

Anxiously "watching the pot" has become its own slow, self-inflicted torture.

How do we escape?

Start with prayer. Pray that the Holy Spirit would command your heart and mind, and keep your attention focused on the things you can control in the here and now.

And when the eyes of your heart and mind drift back to the pot, pray again. Write or print out a key memory verse about waiting on the Lord, and keep it on hand so you can trust in God's timing. I recommend Psalm 27:14: "Wait for the Lord; be strong and take heart and wait for the Lord."

For some, the "watched pot" of marriage is practically irresistible. As a friend to many single women, I've witnessed this firsthand. These friends often stress about the next date, who's noticing them, or why they can't seem to meet anyone. They are educated, self-sufficient, sports-loving, and attractive—in short, I-N-D-E-P-E-N-D-E-N-T women who have everything in the world, but no one to share it with.

I understand their impatience—and the struggles of men who also long for marriage—yet I've come to appreciate the wisdom of looking away from the "pot" and giving it to the Lord. I often advise my friends to focus less on the ticking clock and more on other fulfilling aspects of their lives. If you stop everything in life to wait for something to come to a boil, you'll end up sabotaging it.

Think about it: How many married friends tell you that they met their spouse "when they weren't even looking," or when they'd given up on dating?

For me, dozens. It happens all the time. We're naturally more attractive to others when we're not trying so hard!

Staying patient doesn't mean doing nothing; it means making the most of the present while we await the future.

You can't waste your time as a single person staring at the pot—instead, use this season in your Kitchen to stir your gifts, taste your purpose, and trust God's timing for the feast ahead.

As we'll learn about soon, singleness is where God seasons you with character, patience, and joy that lasts. It's the time to maximize your spiritual growth, personal development, relational capital, financial stewardship, and emotional/mental health. If more of us had done this, our current status, whether married or not, would be so much better!

So don't be afraid to let things simmer. Focus instead on growth, preparation, and self-improvement. And when the moment finally arrives, we'll be ready for it, having spent our time wisely and purposefully.

"Don't Bite Off More Than You Can Chew"

Taking on too many responsibilities at once can lead to exhaustion and decreased effectiveness. Balancing multiple roles, such as writing a book, expanding a business, and maintaining family commitments, requires self-awareness and prioritization.

Luke 12:48 reminds us, "For unto whomsoever much is given, of him shall be much required."

I have kept this kitchen cliché front-of-mind in this season of my life. As I write this chapter, I can't help but think about the last two and half years of preparation and sitting still. After so long, I reached a "boiling point" and several endeavors have culminated all at once: Writing this book, being a real estate investor, expanding my non-profit organization, and growing my consulting business.

Not only that, I'm simultaneously continuing to serve as a wife, assistant pastor, and itinerant preacher.

All are converging. Each is a significant challenge. I've certainly bit off a lot, and it's much more than I could have handled when I was younger!

The complexity of managing these responsibilities requires me to take inventory of my life daily to ensure that I am not overextending myself. Each day, I consciously evaluate my commitments and prioritize my tasks to maintain a balance that allows me to achieve my goals without overwhelming myself.

What are the talents that you have been given to do something with? The key is remembering that you have not been given more than you can handle.

Yet when a new opportunity arises—a new recipe or ingredient—be sure to take stock of your resources: Time, energy, space, and finances. Prayerfully commit these tangible goods to the Lord's purposes. It's completely possible that He will bless the meager resources in your hands and multiply them, just as Jesus did with fishes and loaves. It's also possible He will lead you away from this new opportunity by His Spirit, using the moment to teach you an important lesson about walking with Him.

There is no rule here, nothing I can write that will cover all situations. It's between you and the Spirit just how much you can truly "bite off and chew."

The only way to know for sure is to stay deeply rooted in Him, and in no one and nothing else.

"Don't Put All Your Eggs in One Basket"

It's tempting to go "all-in" on a single plan, resource, or opportunity. I'm sure you've stood at the precipice of a choice that seemed "too good to be true" and couldn't help yourself but jump in.

Yet we all know how dangerous this is. If all the eggs are in a single basket, and that basket falls to the ground, every single egg is done for. It's basic logic.

That's why this cliché is so well-known and applied to so many diverse contexts: Diversifying investments; relationships; career pursuits; exercise; you name it.

The idea of spreading your risk around ensures stability and allows for greater adaptability when unforeseen challenges arise.

Placing all of our hopes, resources, or efforts into one singular plan can leave us vulnerable when unexpected circumstances arise. Just as a well-balanced meal requires a variety of ingredients to enhance flavor and nutrition, our lives benefit from diversification—spreading our talents, investments, and relationships across different opportunities to ensure stability and resilience.

"You Put Your Foot in That Dish"

This Southern expression signifies when someone cooks a dish that is delicious and well-prepared, implying that they have poured their heart and soul into it.

Translating this to life, the phrase serves as a metaphor for putting forth maximum effort, dedication, and passion in everything we do. Whether in careers, relationships, or personal growth, striving for excellence and taking pride in our work allows us to create something extraordinary.

Whether in life or the kitchen, true success comes from being fully present and invested in our actions, transforming the ordinary into something exceptional.

Not only is this wise; it's honoring to God.

In every endeavor, devote the same level of commitment and enthusiasm as you would to Him. Take pride in your work and show genuine care in every detail.

This cliché reminds us that true success and fulfillment come from putting in the work and being fully present in our actions. By doing so, we create something valuable and transformative, not just for ourselves but for those around us.

Yes, decisions in the kitchen—and in life—can be risky. But we are still called to give our absolute best to them, as if we were cooking for the King of Kings Himself.

Trust the Process

Despite understanding these principles, life often presents moments of doubt and struggle. The challenge lies in balancing preparation with faith, trusting the process even when results are not immediate. It's easy to become discouraged when progress seems slow, but just like a dish that needs time to cook, life's breakthroughs often require patience and perseverance.

I experienced this first hand after leaving my athletic coaching career. Coaching had been my only professional identity up to that point, and I had no clear plan for what would come next. That season felt like an eternity. I questioned whether I had made the right decision and wrestled with uncertainty.

I was also grieved by this change. Sports and coaching draw a level of emotion out of me that I can't get anywhere else. There's something about watching others devote themselves to a goal and go to battle for it. By moving on, I inevitably had to turn my face away from coaching toward something else. No one wants to turn their back on an opportunity in life, but there's no other way to answer a call or act out of necessity. And once you move on from something, you always have those little things that you desperately miss.

Thankfully, my waiting period was filled with the "aroma" of unexpected opportunities that sustained me until the right door finally opened—just as in the kitchen.

Those months were not wasted time, but a period of refining, realigning, and equipping me for what was ahead. This season was a test of patience, faith, and my ability to trust that, in due time, the right opportunity would present itself.

The outcome of this wait was better than I expected. However, if I had jumped into another coaching position or taken any job simply to make ends meet, I would have missed an outcome that elevated me financially, challenged me professionally, and positioned me to use the skills that had been lying dormant in my life.

This is why it is crucial that you trust the process.

Don't watch the pot.

And don't crank up the temperature to cook things faster.

As David writes in Psalm 37:7, "Be still in the presence of the Lord, and wait patiently for him to act."

It can be tempting to force a situation to unfold on our timeline, but doing so may lead to unintended consequences. By embracing faith over impatience, we recognize that every step in our journey—every challenge, every delay, every detour—is part of God's greater plan. Just as a carefully prepared meal requires intentionality, our lives require trust and obedience. Choosing to lean into the process rather than resist it brings peace and fulfillment.

The kitchen serves as a powerful symbol of the way preparation, patience, and wisdom are key ingredients in both cooking and life.

Whether we are waiting for water to boil, choosing which voices to listen to, or deciding how much we can realistically handle, we are constantly learning and growing.

This renovation specifically targets our expectations, making it an especially difficult one. It can be easier to look around and, like the Living Room, decide that it is other people's faults for not communicating well. But in the Kitchen, it's all about how well you endure the heat of risky decisions.

Can you stand firm despite the rising temperatures? Do you trust the Lord to renovate your tolerance for uncertainty?

This is why we must learn to trust the process. Only by doing so—and by embracing the lessons life provides us afterward—can we position ourselves to experience what God has in store for us. As we read in James 1:4, "Let perseverance finish its work so that you may be mature and complete, not lacking anything."

Questions for Reflection

1. Think of a time when you felt like you were in a season of preparation. How did you handle the waiting period, and what did you learn from it?

2. Reflecting on the phrase "a watched pot never boils," in what areas of your life are you struggling with impatience? How can you shift your focus while trusting that the process is still unfolding?

3. What is one practical step you can take this week to better prepare for the next season of your life?

Journaling Prompt

Consider a moment when God's timing was different from your own plans. What was the outcome, and how did it shape your faith?

My Prayer for You

Father,

Thank You that You are the Provider—the One who brings nourishment, warmth, and creation into the spaces where we break bread, where we consider our calling, where risk simmers like a pot on the stove. I pray now for the person standing before the kitchen of the soul: For the dreams they've ignored, the ingredients of their life they've left raw, the fear that keeps the stove unlit.

Lord, bring Your fire and Your recipe into this place. Stir in Your courage where there is hesitation. Let Your flavor of purpose season their plans. Strip out the stale habits, the leftovers of fear, the half-trusted gifts. And let new risk rise: Risk of offering, risk of failing, risk of hope.

May this room become their lab of transformation—where they taste Your goodness and release their limiting fears. Let it be a space where creativity and faith bake together, where the nourishment of their soul is prepared and shared. Bless the table they will set—whether for one or many—and show them that You have more than crumbs: You have a feast.

In Jesus' Name, Amen

Kid's Room

The Room of Becoming and Belonging

> *"Truly I tell you, unless you change and become like little children, you will never enter the kingdom of heaven."* — Matthew 18:3 (NIV)

When you're a kid, Christmas is the highlight of the year. For me it wasn't just the gifts—though the gifts were a huge part of it—but the way our house would fill up with people. My grandmother had twelve children, which meant I was bound to have a stack of gifts under the tree by the time everyone visited.

I would constantly survey the prickly pine tree each time one of my aunts or uncles came by, eagerly checking if my gift pile grew.

One year, my Uncle Charles came by early—much earlier than usual. I was confused. If he was coming early, did that mean he wouldn't be back for Christmas? Would I miss out on a gift?

As his kids came into the house, I immediately went outside to play with my cousin Jackie, and I immediately noticed something was different: She was carrying the coolest red bag I had ever seen. It was a child's suitcase with Mickey Mouse on it, and in my eight-year-old mind it symbolized *possibility*. She could go anywhere in the world because *she had luggage*.

As our playtime progressed and we moved to the front porch, I overheard my uncle telling my grandmother that he was taking his kids to Disney World. Suddenly, that red bag became even more powerful. It wasn't just a cute accessory—it was a ticket to adventure, fun, and memories.

Soon, I realized my uncle was getting ready to leave. He wouldn't be back for Christmas, he explained to Mama, which is why he visited early.

Uh oh, I thought. *If he isn't returning, I'm going to be short a gift this year!*

But to my surprise, my uncle began persuading my grandmother to let me travel to Disney World with him and his kids. Her first response was that she didn't have the money to send me, but my uncle assured her that he had it all under control—he just really wanted me to go.

One would think this moment would be euphoric for me. However, there was a detail I couldn't get over, and it somehow crushed my spirit into crumbs: I didn't have my own red bag.

I should have been doing cartwheels from the excitement, but I instead felt small and ashamed. There was something about my cousin's red Mickey Mouse bag that made her special in my eyes. That bag somehow made her worthy of a trip to Disney World.

But I didn't have a red bag. In fact, I didn't have *any* bag. I'd never even been on a vacation before.

So despite the words my uncle was saying, and the reality that the grown-ups around me could easily have solved this problem, my heart had already decided that I wasn't going, that I *couldn't* go, and I was tumbling into a deep chasm of relentless despair.

Nothing could pull me out, either. Mama quickly turned around and agreed to let my uncle take me on the vacation. Still I sat on the edge of my bed, crying, paralyzed by insecurity. My uncle offered to help me pack, but I couldn't move. I was frozen. Mama, in her typical no-nonsense fashion, began offering solutions suitable for her sensibilities: Paper bags, duffle bags, plastic bags—even her satin-lined suitcase.

But none of it felt right. In my mind, without a red bag—the kind of bag a daughter of my uncle would possess—I didn't qualify.

You might think this is a small thing, but it shaped how I looked at myself.

As I lay across my childhood bed, eyes blinded with stinging tears, I felt like an orphan. Abandoned and unloved—all because my heart had decided that there was an object that would make me *someone* versus no one.

To Belong

I almost didn't hear my uncle ask me what was wrong. When he said it, I couldn't answer, only shake my head.

Meanwhile, Mama was becoming more and more impatient because, from her point of view, I was wasting time.

But Uncle Charles was putting things together. He left the room without a word while Mama continued to try to inspire me to get off my behind and start packing. Then he reappeared.

"I hope you know I wouldn't forget *your* Christmas present," he said.

In his arms was a large, beautifully wrapped gift.

I blinked, trying to push the tears away so I could tell if what I was seeing was truly happening.

Yes, there it is. A gift for me!

I managed a half-smile between my swollen, tear-blanched cheeks, and sat up on the side of the bed.

"Open it," he insisted.

I set on that box like a pack of wolves attacking a wounded rabbit. Paper flew in the air and the room was filled with the near-deafening *rip! rip! rip!* of my anxious tearing.

Then I saw what Uncle Charles had gotten me.

My own red bag.

It had wheels, like adult suitcases. And on the side, both Mickey *and* Minne Mouse beamed at me, their cartoon smiles the most beautiful thing I'd ever seen.

At the sight of it—my own red bag—I cried even harder, and possibly passed out for a minute. I don't honestly remember, that moment is a blur of emotions.

But in that instant, my uncle unknowingly showed me how to see myself in a different light. I'll never know what would have come of me if that day hadn't happened.

It wasn't jealousy, either. I didn't want Jackie's bag. I didn't want my grandmother's satin-lined bag, either.

I wanted a bag of my own—a bag that said I belonged. I wanted to feel like I belonged in a way that said, *You can go anywhere and do anything.* No more hoping for someone or something to qualify me to take steps or opportunities.

We all long for a "red bag" moment. A time when someone sees us in our weakness or inability, and then reaches out in love to welcome us into the fold. When you're suddenly included and viewed as a complete person.

Memories or Traumas?

The kid's room is a peculiar place in the home.

For a season it is a child's haven. They pass through numerous phases and fads, and the neglected spaces often end up cluttered with debris and dust from last year's obsession. Dolls, drawings, pieces of a toy set.

Then a time comes when the Kid's Room is no longer *just* the room where a child lives. It might become an office or guest room. It might get renovated into a larger room or living space.

Unlike the other rooms of the house, the Kid's Room undergoes the most transformation in the shortest span of time; it is the place where one becomes someone else, yet always longs to feel like they belong to the house as a whole.

We all grow up, but we never truly outgrow the memories of childhood.

In the "house" of your spirit, much of your childhood remains. These remnants may be renovated, stored in boxes, or stuffed into closets; but they are still a core part of your identity, and we must learn their lessons if we wish to live healthy, joyful lives.

The Kid's Room isn't just the room for little humans to play; it is the sacred space of becoming, growing, transforming, and eventually departing. It may be a part of your distant past, but it is still a part of your House, and like the other rooms, it requires your careful attention.

Whether your recollections are mostly composed of delightful memories, staggering traumas, or something in between, the aging pieces of your Kid's Room are crucial elements of who you are, who you were, and who you are about to become.

A Room Full of Emotions

Isn't it interesting how a child enters their room as a baby in a crib and, before you know it, they're sleeping in a twin-sized bed—maybe even a bunk bed if they're lucky?

I was an only child with twin beds in my room growing up, but I always wanted a bunk bed. To be honest, even in my 40s, I still wouldn't mind having one!

As a child matures into their teenage years, their bed is upgraded again—this time to a full or queen-sized bed.

The Kid's Room witnesses every stage of transition: Infancy to adolescence, late-night tears to belly-laughs with friends, toys scattered on the floor to posters of pop stars and athletes hanging on the wall. And as the room shifts, so do the layers of the person inside it. The Kid's Room isn't just a space—it's a snapshot of seasons, transitions, identity, and even silent struggles.

As parents, or as former children ourselves, we often decorate a child's room based on what they love at the moment. The theme might be superheroes, princesses, sports, or science. But behind every design choice is a reflection of the child's current stage of development. And sometimes, when the child can't decide for themselves, the parents step in and try to create a space that reflects what *they* think their child needs.

Either way, these changing decorations tell a story.

As I grew, those toys made room for posters of Michael Jackson, Prince, Janet Jackson, and New Edition. Glow-in-the-dark stars dotted my ceiling, while Michael Jordan and Magic Johnson smiled down from the walls.

Toys tell the story, too. I vividly remember getting a Black Barbie doll and feeling such a deep sense of pride and representation. Toy chests overflowed with stuffed animals like teddy bears and My Little Ponies, each with its own backstory and personality. These weren't just toys; they were companions, protectors, and storytellers of my inner world.

Each one of us had a room—shared or solo—that became more than just a bedroom. It was our cultural sanctuary. The boombox became sacred, blasting LL Cool J, TLC, and Run-DMC, while mixtapes became the love letters of our generation.

Remember making a mixtape for your crush? I sure do!

And if you were *really* fancy, you had a personal TV and VCR. I used mine to record music videos on VHS and watch them over and over like they were live performances.

It's fun to look back on the decor, the vibes, and the energy of our kid rooms, but more importantly, it's a reminder of the *moments* that shaped who we are. Our interests never defined us, but our passion about them did. We learned not just what to love, but what it meant to love something or someone. To be loyal and to feel betrayed.

Parents can especially appreciate the fact that children's interests are always changing. The favorite brand, show, or band of the moment can quickly become a faux pas. Something new swoops in to take its place, sending anxious parents back to the store to update the wardrobe or toy chest.

Change is central to our lives, yet as adults we tend to resist it. As we learned in the Kitchen, I resisted leaving my career as a track and field coach for several months. That position had come to define me.

Children go through this process too, but at lightspeed. They want to belong to the right group, to be included with the best people.

Eight-year-old me wanted this, too. Without my father in the picture, I desperately wanted to be welcomed by a strong, loving paternal figure. That was my uncle.

That's why in that moment, sitting there clutching my red bag, I felt seen, known, and loved. That red bag became more than just an accessory; it was a quiet declaration. It spoke of possibility, of movement, of identity. It made me feel like maybe I belonged somewhere beyond that hallway.

But the little girl in me still had questions. Still wondered if she was enough. Still didn't understand why she longed for more or felt different in ways she couldn't name. There were fears tucked behind that smile, doubts sitting just beneath the surface. Even as that moment marked something powerful, I was still very much in process—still just a child trying to make sense of the world around me.

That's why the Kids Room holds a sacred tension between becoming and just being.

It walks a tightrope stretched between the child's need to be nurtured and the early whispers of purpose calling out from the corners of innocence. It's a place where identity begins to take root, even when confidence hasn't fully bloomed.

Who you are now is intimately connected to the changes that took place in your own "Kid's Room." The choices you made; the risks you took; the errors and sins you committed; all of it forms a narrative thread that declares to you whether or not you belong.

This is why we must carefully determine how to renovate the Kid's Rooms of our hearts. Despite years of neglect or hiding, our past is still there.

It is a room full of dominos that, if tipped over, could start a cascade of tumultuous emotions.

And if poorly managed, those emotions could defeat and destroy you.

There Is No Perfect Kid's Room

Psychologists have much to say about trauma; some, like Sigmund Freud, think it is paramount in the formation of the self. Others, like Alfred Adler, argue that moments of "trauma" are actually critical decision-making points where we make subconscious choices about securing our own happiness.

Regardless of which perspective is more in fashion, or more widely held by the scientific community, one thing between them is true:

Painful moments in early life become ground zero for our identity.

This is why the Kid's Room is paradoxical: It *should* be a safe haven for youthful play and innocence, but it isn't. It can't be. In this world of tragedy, brutality, and unspeakable crimes against children, there is no completely safe space where kids won't be somehow traumatized.

And even if you were able to create the perfect Kid's Room—some hermetically sealed paradise with no intrusions or villainy from outside—sin and darkness would emerge from within.

"Then Jesus called to the crowd to come and hear," Mark writes in Chapter 7 of his gospel. "'All of you listen,' he said, 'and try to understand. It's not what goes into your body that defiles you; you are defiled by what comes from your heart,'" (Mark 7:14–15).

Jesus isn't speaking in a vacuum, either. Hundreds of years earlier, the prophet Jeremiah wrote, "The human heart is the most deceitful of all things, and desperately wicked. Who really knows how bad it is?" (Jeremiah 17:9).

The truth is that we are traumatized from within and without; we are corrupted and led astray by myriad forces pulling on our passions from every direction. You could attempt to protect yourself or your children from the evil world; many people do. Yet what happens in many cases? Some "sheltered" kids end up rebelling anyway, pushing against boundaries to discover the world for themselves.

Should we seek to protect our little ones from the many dangers that hunt them? Of course! To not do so is irresponsible.

But we must not be surprised that, in many cases of childhood resistance and defiance, the call will be coming from inside the house. The loss of innocence isn't due to an invasion, but an insurrection. That which comes from the heart is what truly defiles.

Healing From the Decay

There is a mysterious and grievous decay of the Kid's Room that occurs over the course of time. Healing from this decomposition is a slow and ongoing process that requires us to trust in God's wisdom.

It's easy to look at the fall of the Kid's Room and think, *God's not in control. How could He allow "that thing" to have happened to me, or to my loved one when we were young and innocent?*

Decomposition is the devil's basic vocabulary. It's the slow grind with which he assaults our hope, optimism, and faith. We must make ourselves aware of it and push back.

However, the way to protect your youthful hope isn't to ignore what happened to your Kid's Room, but to stare it full in the face and allow yourself to process all that took place there.

Look long and hard at how time eroded it; how time aged you out of naivete and into stark awareness of how the world *really* works.

Look at the things you cherished as a younger person—the toys, the dolls, the posters, the love letters, the outfits—and see how they are now faded, tattered, dust-caked, and smeared with dirt.

Look at the space that was supposed to be completely safe, and consider how that sanctity was ruined, whether by an invader or the intrusive thoughts polluting your own mind.

These wounds do not simply disappear with time. Like the neglected spaces in our homes, they slowly rot, mold, or decompose. Only when we pull away the trappings of adult life and expose what lies hidden beneath can we begin to deal with that is really at the heart of our spiritual houses.

This isn't happening to you because you are uniquely flawed or broken; this is *universal*. All of use see this in our houses—and specifically in the Kid's Room where our childhood hurts still echo.

Like a neglected leak, infestation, or crack in your foundation, fractures in our spiritual homes do not magically go away; they evolve and shift into critical threats to our mental, spiritual, and even physical wellbeing as adults.

The question is: Have you taken the time and energy to heal from your own loss of innocence? Have you been able to forgive others for what they did to you?

And have you been able to come to the Lord in surrender and trust that in spite of it all, He is still incredibly good?

Forgive Yourself

Then consider the secrets you kept as a child, and the embarrassment you felt and tried to hide. Was it about being caught naked while changing clothes? Was it that your parents would find a note you'd written to a crush, or a letter that crush had passed to you?

Was it dolls or toys or cars that you didn't want others to find out about, and shoved under the bed to keep out of the light?

The things you hid as a child are probably the things you're hiding today.

It may not be a seventh grade love letter, but it may be an emotional tryst with a colleague. Throughout our lives, we tend to scratch the same itch, over and over. How have your childhood longings "grown up?"

You may not be hiding a toy that you "borrowed" from a friend or the store, with no intention of returning; but it could be a possession you "have to have" but don't want your spouse or children to know about. Alcohol. Expensive electronics. A gun.

We ache to possess the things we crave and covet. Yet we feel tremendous shame for acquiring them without full honesty or transparency, and just as we did in our childhood, we'll hide them in dark places and pray our loved ones don't discover the truth.

A friend and fellow Christ-follower has a saying he uses with teenagers to warn them about this process:

"You don't grow out of your bad habits; they become your defining character traits."

Whatever happened in your room as a kid hasn't simply stopped; whoever you were in the Kid's Room hasn't magically vanished or transformed into someone else. You're still you!

Now the question is whether you have undertaken the process of forgiving yourself. I'm certain you've beaten yourself up plenty over these mistakes; have you given them to God and trusted that His grace is sufficient in your weakness?

Only then can we free ourselves from the pangs of childhood and adolescent sin that reverberate through the rest of our lives.

Growing With Patience and Peace

If we ever hope to enjoy spiritual maturity and lasting peace with God, we must *make peace* with the wounds in our past.

That doesn't mean we ignore the hurts done to us; it doesn't mean we bypass justice or enable abusers. Quite to the contrary, in fact. Forgiveness doesn't give wrongdoers carte blanche to carry on with their crimes.

But it does mean that we forgive: Forgive those who wronged us, and forgive ourselves. For all abuse and trauma tells the lie that "it's your fault."

This is why walking into your old room—even in memories and dreams—can stir up such emotion. The Kid's Room is a time capsule of many paradoxical things: Innocence; optimism; self-doubt; loneliness; joy and laughter; agonizing pain. This room embodies your entire life on a continuum. It *was* you and yet wasn't completely; it *is* you, and yet hardly encompasses the totality of who you are.

Take a moment to pause. Reflect on the road that lay behind you, however crooked and broken it may be.

How was God present in all of it, even when things seemed hopeless and bleak? How has God sweetened the bitter wounds of days past?

The answers to these Kid's Room questions are the path to one of our ultimate goals: Spiritual maturity, and with it, spiritual freedom.

The Bible speaks about spiritual maturity in ways similar to psychological growth: It's a process.

We are called to grow and mature in our faith, but that doesn't mean we bypass the foundational steps. Just as a child cannot skip from a crib to a queen-sized bed without proper growth, neither can we move too quickly into spiritual maturity without laying a proper foundation.

In 1 Peter 2:2, the apostle writes, "Like newborn babies, crave pure spiritual milk, so that by it you may grow up in your salvation." The progression of growth from infancy to maturity is not something we can rush. If we fail to nurture our spiritual foundations, our growth will be stunted. We must be intentional about our spiritual nourishment, understanding that each season of life has something to teach us.

The Kid's Room reminds us that our spiritual lives, like our childhood development, require patience. We cannot skip over the stages where we are meant to learn how to rely on God, develop trust, and seek His guidance. Just as the child in the crib cannot rush into adulthood, neither can we skip steps in our relationship with God.

Think about where *you* might be rushing your own spiritual growth, or the growth of someone in your life.

What parts of your life or faith journey are you trying to fast-track? In Philippians 1:6, Paul says, "Being confident of this, that he who began a good work in you will carry it on to completion until the day of Christ Jesus."

There's no need to rush things because our God is a patient God, and He allows us to grow at the pace He has set. He is not anxious about us; it is we who are anxious and constantly hurrying.

Additionally, take time to think about moments in your childhood when you were forced to develop too quickly, or according to someone else's expectations or timetable.

When were you forced to abandon a "phase" that you weren't quite ready to let go of? What were the benefits of this, and what lingering wounds might you still be carrying?

How were you put into an age-inappropriate role—like acting as the "confidante" of your parent, rather than as a child—and required to act much older than you were ready?

As you can probably tell, these questions are bound to stir up deeply hurtful and traumatic memories. Abuse is a scourge on young people all across the world. These are great questions to explore with trained professionals who can help you process, navigate, and heal from the wounds.

Don't try to answer these questions entirely on your own, either. Peter calls Satan "a roaring lion" who prowls about, looking for weak or isolated prey. It's when we try to walk this troublesome road on our own that he is primed to strike.

We'll address these questions and more soon, but feel free to take the time you need to reach out to Him as memories of your Kid's Room come into your mind.

Finding Hope Again

Mark 9:14-29 gives us a way to answer these difficult questions, both as a story of miraculous healing and a lesson in spiritual maturation.

In this passage, Jesus finds His disciples arguing with a group of religious leaders, surrounded by a crowd. A man from the crowd steps forward and explains that he has brought his son to the disciples to be healed of a terrible affliction: Demonic possession. The boy is tormented by an evil spirit that renders him mute and causes violent seizures. The disciples are unable to heal him, and the father, desperate, turns to Jesus.

"How long has this been happening to him?" Jesus asks. This question might seem strange in such an urgent moment, but it is incredibly important. There are things in all of our lives—past pain, struggles, and deep-seated doubts—that trace all the way back to our childhoods. Whether good, bad, or indifferent, these memories shape who we are, even as adults.

The father answers: "Since he was a little boy. The spirit often throws him into the fire or into water, trying to kill him."

Since he was a little boy.

Think about that. This is the kind of detail we tend to breeze past as we read, eager to get to the inevitable messianic miracle.

But stop and think about that: This young man has been tortured by a demon since childhood. Since he was young, innocent, and naive.

What the heck happened to *that* Kid's Room? Think of the way this man's youth was completely destroyed by forces from within and without!

But it's not just the boy who's suffering. The father, too, is in turmoil. His response to Jesus is a mixture of belief and doubt: "Have mercy on us and help us, if you can."

This father's vulnerability is striking. In the midst of such desperation, he doesn't hide his doubts. In all the gospels, he is the only one who questions Jesus's ability—not His willingness—to help.

Let that sink in: This father doubted whether Jesus could help him and his son. The ravages of the world had destroyed the father and son's ability to hope anymore. All childhood innocence had been burnt to ashes by Satan's torment. They had no hope.

Then Jesus comes along, and the father is tempted to believe again.

Jesus was taken aback by the father's words, but had beautiful compassion on the weary father. "What do you mean, 'If I can?'" Jesus asked. "Anything is possible if a person believes."

Then, with all the desperation and agony of a parent wanting to save their child, the father cries out, "I do believe, but help me overcome my unbelief!"

Hopefully you know the rest of the story. Jesus commands the unclean spirit to depart from the boy, and with one last violent spasm, it does so. The boy is so exhausted from the demonic assault that he appears dead, but Jesus takes him by the hand and lifts him up and returns him to his father.

Finally—after years of fighting against the powers of Hell itself—the father and son can rest, all thanks to the power of Jesus Christ.

This poignant story from Mark 9 is easy to quickly read because we know the ending. Of course Jesus casts out the demon. Of course Heaven is victorious.

But the real victory isn't about casting out the demon; it's about healing the father's broken faith.

The loss of childhood innocence—whether your own or that of a loved one—can break us. The questions of sin and evil in youth are never easy. They leave us wondering, *Where was God when....?*

Yet Jesus comes, encourages us to believe, and then heals. He reminds us that there is compassion for the struggling believer and the soul fatigued by the weight of Satan's rule and reign.

Jesus is here for you, no matter how painful or messy your past might be.

If the decay of your Kid's Room is poisoning your faith today, run to Jesus. Ask Him to heal each broken toy, each hidden note, each scar on the floor and scuff on the wall. Believe that His death on the cross and resurrection from the grave are more than sufficient to forgive your past sins, present addictions, and future failures. Believe that He loves you *not* because of your idyllic perfection, but because you are His forever.

Pray, "I believe; help my unbelief!"

Find Your Bag, Find Your Father

I don't know what would have happened to my life if I hadn't gotten that red bag from my uncle. Perhaps things would have turned out just fine; there's truly no way to know.

But I do know what *did* happen: I began the journey of making peace with my childhood and its various wounds.

My mother was hardly ever present for my youth. My father a mystery, that cavernous hole in my sense of self. The hushed secrets about my grandmother's health. The general wounds that emerge from growing up in a messed up world wracked with Satan's lies and cruel circumstances.

The gift of that bag changed everything. It countered the main lie Satan was using to torment me, that *I didn't belong.* No one wanted me, and while I was being cared for, it was only a matter of time until the people in my life found a good enough reason to cast me off. This lie warped me and bent my heart into a self-defeating pretzel. In ways, it still does.

But the gift of the bag said, *That's not true. You* do *belong, and you belong to* me.

My uncle didn't realize the gravity of the message behind his Christmas present. Yet it worked a miracle in my spirit. It began filling in the father-shaped hole in my heart.

More than that, it mimicked the sacrificial love of Jesus Christ. I was no daughter to him at all. Sure, I was a niece, but he had no obligation to get me the same gift as his very own daughter, or to take me on a lavish vacation alongside her. He was treating me as if I was his daughter, too!

This is the power of God's adoptive grace, purchased by the blood of Jesus on the cross and activated by His glorious resurrection from the grave: We are no longer orphans, cut off by our rebellion and sin. We are sons and daughters of the King of Kings!

The Apostle Paul writes in his letter to the Romans: "So you have not received a spirit that makes you fearful slaves. Instead, you received God's Spirit when he adopted you as his own children. Now we call him, 'Abba, Father.' For his Spirit joins with our spirit to affirm that we are God's children. And since we are his children, we are his heirs," (Romans 8:15–17).

My uncle made this Scripture come alive for me. He didn't redeem me the way Jesus Christ redeems me, but he gave me a taste of the eternal joy that is mine in my Lord.

So let me ask you: What is *your* red bag story? What moment in your story began the journey of revealing God's adoptive love?

If you can't think of one right now, don't worry. In just a moment, you'll have the chance to reflect and hopefully uncover a piece of your own story that will bring you hope and lasting joy.

Remember: The Kid's Room reminds us that every stage of growth matters. Spiritually, we must revisit these rooms and ask: What part of me is still a child waiting to be seen? What lies did I accept at an early age that I now carry as truth? And how can I nurture the young places within me that still need healing?

Whether you're raising children or learning to re-parent your younger self, know this—God sees every stage. He is not rushing you. He's not disappointed in your process. He wants to sit with you in the Kid's Room and remind you: *You are safe. You are loved. And it's okay to grow at your own pace.*

Questions for Reflection

1. What "red bag" moments have you experienced, where someone's loving action made you feel seen, known, and loved? How did these moments impact your sense of belonging and identity?

2. Reflect on your own "Kid's Room." What memories, both joyful and painful, are stored there? How have these childhood experiences shaped who you are today?

3. What lies about your worth or identity, stemming from childhood experiences, might you still be carrying as truth? How can you begin to challenge these lies and nurture the "young places within you that still need healing"?

Journaling Prompt

Is there a part of your childhood or adolescent experience that still needs healing? How might you bring that to Jesus, just as the father brought his son?

My Prayer for You

Father,

Thank You for the gift of childhood, the beauty of transition, and the innocence that shapes us into who You've called us to be. Just as the Kid's Room is a space of change, where we learn, grow, and sometimes struggle, I pray for each person reading this chapter. I ask that You would gently guide them through their own transitions, whether they are stepping into new seasons of life or reflecting on the ones that have passed.

Lord, help us to hold onto the sweetness of nostalgia, even as we move away from the simplicity and innocence of childhood. Remind us that You are with us through every stage of growth—through the joy of discovery and the pain of change. Just like the red bag in my own story, may we recognize the moments in our lives where You have shaped us, where You have spoken to our hearts, and where You've been present even in the smallest of details.

For anyone feeling lost or unsure in the midst of transition, I pray for Your peace and guidance. Let them see that every stage of life has its purpose, and that even in the awkwardness or uncertainty, You are there, working within them. May they feel Your love and Your invitation to grow with You, through every step of the journey.

In Jesus' Name, Amen

Single Bedroom

The Room of Nakedness and Trust

"You know when I sit down or stand up. You know my thoughts even when I'm far away." —Psalm 139:2

"Where the bedroom is wrong, the whole house is wrong."

It's where you sleep. Where you change clothes. Where you go to cry, pray, meditate, or reveal your deepest longings.

It's the room where you make terrible mistakes, and where you share life's most precious connections. Where you beg for death. Where you create life itself.

Where you dream and tumble into the depths of your subconscious, facing the wonders and terrors lurking there.

Where you put yourself together and take yourself apart.

The Bedroom is where you are truly your most naked self—the person you are without any adornment, costume, mask, or status symbol.

It is also a room where our greatest dependencies come to life: Our need for intimacy and connection; our need for solitude and control; our need for purpose and truth.

Author Margaret Kennedy was right: Where the bedroom is wrong, the whole house is wrong.

If we aren't living well in the room of nakedness and dependence, those issues will seep into the entirety of our houses, apartments, flats, condos, or trailers. But they won't stop there; these matters will inexorably spread into our relationships, into our emotional health, into how we carry ourselves in the world.

Bedroom issues are foundational issues, and they must be handled with courage and boldness.

The Room Where Vulnerability Happens

You can tell a lot about someone by their bedroom.

It's the one room in the house where presence often outweighs presentation. More than just a space to sleep, the bedroom becomes the keeper of our deepest vulnerabilities, our truest selves, and sometimes our most fragile secrets.

It's where the day begins and ends, where dreams are born and sometimes where they quietly die.

And it's where intimacy—emotional, spiritual, and physical—takes root or slowly withers.

Throughout history, the bedroom has evolved from a shared communal space into a private haven. The earliest sleeping quarters were born out of necessity—groups of people huddled together for warmth and safety. Over time, as privacy became a cultural value, the bedroom was carved out as a separate and sacred space. By the Renaissance, the wealthy boasted private chambers. By the modern era, even children had rooms of their own.

This shift tells us something: The need for a place to retreat, reflect, and reconnect isn't just a luxury—it's deeply human.

RENOVATING THE HEART

Carl Sandburg once said, "You remember some bedrooms you have slept in. There are bedrooms you like to remember and others you would like to forget."

Whether the memories bring comfort or discomfort, they linger—proof that the bedroom, unlike any other room, imprints itself on the soul.

Even within cultural traditions, the bedroom is treated with reverence. My grandmother, mama who you met in Chapter 1 had a couple of rules: "Don't let anybody sit on your bed, you don't sit on other people's beds and you don't sit on the bed with your street clothes on." Her tone said what she didn't—this is sacred space. Not because of the furniture or the size of the room, but because of what it represented: Rest, respect, and protection.

And who hasn't chuckled—or winced—at the old saying, "If these walls could talk…." The truth is, if bedroom walls *could* talk, they'd tell stories of love and heartbreak, hope and hopelessness, shame and embarrassment, and prayers whispered into pillows and tears soaked into blankets.

They'd tell the truth—the kind we often can't and won't say out loud.

Then there's that childhood bedtime benediction: "Sleep tight, don't let the bed bugs bite." It sounds playful, almost silly now, but if you listen closely, you can hear something sacred beneath the rhyme. In a world that can be harsh, unpredictable, and unkind, this small phrase became a nightly blessing, a wish for rest without disturbance, safety without intrusion, and peace without fear. It was more than just a way to say goodnight—it was a ritual, a shield of words meant to guard the sanctity of sleep and the sacredness of the space where we lay our heads.

Because the bedroom is not just where we sleep—it's where we surrender. It's where we are unguarded.

And that kind of vulnerability requires protection.

Finally, the bedroom is where we are most human. It's where we undress—literally and metaphorically. Where we laugh freely, cry loudly, wrestle out loud with thoughts, make impossible decisions, and sometimes, pursue God—or awake to find Him pursuing us. Whether shared or private, grand or modest, it remains the most intimate room in the house.

Given the importance of this room—and its shifting role in singlehood versus marriage—how should we tend to it with intentionality? How ought we go about reclaiming it not only as a space of comfort, but as a sanctuary for healing, truth, and presence?

Because when the bedroom is in order, the rest of the house feels more whole.

The Battlefield of the Bedroom

If your bedroom has ever been a battlefield—emotionally, spiritually, or physically—you're not alone.

For many of us, this room holds our deepest secrets. Things we've never said out loud. Memories we've tried to forget. Moments we've replayed too many times. The betrayal we didn't expect. The conversations that broke us. The touches that weren't tender. The words that weren't kind. The silence that was deafening.

But the good news is this:

God enters rooms we've locked. He redeems places we've abandoned. He heals what's happened in the dark.

He doesn't ask us to pretend the pain didn't happen. He doesn't demand that we ignore the mess behind the bedroom door. He invites us to bring it to Him. To let Him reclaim what was once sacred and restore intimacy not just with others, but with ourselves, and most importantly, with Him.

Scripture is filled with God's desire to meet us in private spaces: "But when you pray, go away by yourself, shut the door behind you, and pray to your Father in private. Then your Father, who sees everything, will reward you," (Matthew 6:6).

This kind of intimacy is sacred. It's not just about romance or relationships—it's about being seen, known, and safe.

Perhaps this is the moment to address the elephant in the Bedroom: Sex.

Sex is a crucial piece of the battle. First of all, God calls us to live pure lives and only use sex in a way that is honoring to Him. Paul teaches, "Run from sexual sin! No other sin so clearly affects the body as this one does. For sexual immorality is a sin against your own body. Don't you realize that your body is the temple of the Holy Spirit, who lives in you and was given to you by God? You do not belong to yourself, for God bought you with a high price. So you must honor God with your body," (1 Corinthians 6:18–20).

Yet winning the battle against sexual immorality is incredibly difficult. We live in a culture drenched in sexualization. Companies use it to sell their products. Celebrities and influencers lean on it to build their brands. Explicit images and videos have never been so easily accessed, including by very young people who are not physically or emotionally mature enough to process what they're seeing.

While sexual sin isn't a part of everyone's story, it is a widespread reality, *especially* amongst Christ followers and those who call themselves adopted sons and daughters of God.

And few sins play into Satan's strategy more than sexual ones, because they produce the ultimate isolating emotion: Shame.

The battlefield of the bedroom isn't a battlefield of sex; it's a war against shame.

It's the campaign to keep Satan from gaining the ultimate foothold in your spirit.

If you want to live a life of joy, peace, and transformational intimacy, you must do what it takes to evict shame from your spirit; you must be willing to renovate a room where nothing is guaranteed to get better.

However, our enemy is clever, and doing this isn't going to be easy.

Overcoming Shame

Shame is the first sign of sin; it's also a warning sign that we're about to flee from God.

History's first couple, Adam and Eve, experienced this exact thing when they first disobeyed God's instructions: "At that moment their eyes were opened, and they suddenly felt **shame** at their nakedness. So they sewed fig leaves together to cover themselves," (Genesis 3:7, emphasis added).

Neither had committed a sexual sin, but they had done something in direct opposition to God's perfect way. This act exposed them, creating a brand new sensation: Nakedness. And with nakedness came shame.

We are no different. The very idea of being seen naked is the ultimate embarrassment; surely you've had the dream that you showed up to school or work without any pants on. I certainly have, and it's the worst!

Here's the thing:

When we sin or end up in an embarrassing situation, we may *feel* shame; that does not mean God is *ashamed* of us.

Shame is the red flag that Satan is trying to separate us from our loving Father. He has capitalized on a weakness of ours—a temptation, blind spot, or bad coincidence—and is about to pounce by making us feel exactly what Adam and Eve felt.

Never does he do this more than with sex.

Our single years are often plagued with sexual sin and the temptation to commit it. Even if we don't indulge the impulses of our bodies, we still fall short in our thoughts. Unfortunately, limiting sexual rebellion to our fantasies isn't the parachute we think it is.

In His Sermon on the Mount, Jesus teaches, "You have heard the commandment that says, 'You must not commit adultery.' But I say, anyone who even looks at a woman with lust has already committed adultery with her in his heart," (Matthew 5:27–28).

The truth is that sexual purity is hopelessly out of reach for practically every one of us. This isn't to say we should abandon its pursuit—holiness is the ideal we should seek after, no matter what. But to rest on our sexual purity, and somehow trust in it to deliver us, is a fallacy. As Paul writes, quoting the Psalms, "No one is righteous—not even one. No one is truly wise; no one is seeking God. All have turned away; all have become useless," (Romans 3:10–12).

This is why we must trust that God is not ashamed of us. When we confess that Jesus died to pay the penalty for our sins, we no longer trust in our own righteousness, sexual or otherwise. Instead, we trade the filthy rag of our purity for His glorious blood, poured out on our behalf. We trust that His grace is sufficient, since our ability to achieve worldly holiness is not, nor ever will be.

This is difficult for many to accept, but perhaps not for the reason you're thinking.

For if you lived, or are living, a sexually pure life outside of marriage, you might read that and think, "That's not fair!"

And if you've lived, or are living, a sexually wayward life outside of marriage, you probably read that and think, "That's not possible!"

To both of these responses, there is only one answer, again from the Apostle Paul: "I no longer count on my own righteousness through obeying the law; rather, I become righteous through faith in Christ. For God's way of making us right with himself depends on faith," (Phillipians 3:9).

Our righteousness comes through faith in Jesus Christ, *not* **through following some strict code.**

That doesn't give any of us license to wildly sin and treat Jesus's blood as a trivial thing; doing so is, in fact, quite dangerous and blasphemous.

But when we repent of our sins—both the sins of promiscuity and self-righteousness—God is faithful to forgive us and sanctify us.

Otherwise, we become slaves to sin and shame: Either as the slave himself, or the slavemaster, dealing out punishments and insults to those we believe are less than us.

Either way, Satan wins his slaves and chains us to a broken system with no hope and no peace. I don't want this for myself or for anyone I love, and I hope you can see the beauty in God's better, holy way!

We cannot allow the Bedroom to become a place of shame. And if yours already has, there is hope in the redeeming gospel of Jesus Christ to purify it, perform the kind of heavenly renovation we can only dream of, and transform it into something gloriously beautiful.

So how do we conquer shame? How do we redeem the broken pieces of our most intimate selves?

The answer is simple: Understand who you are willing to "get naked" with, and why.

Intimacy is Trust

Satan has been threatening us with exposure since the dawn of time. It is his primary strategy and it has been enormously successful.

When I think about the Bedroom, and the fact that it is the only room in the house where we are naked and *not* trying to clean or cleanse ourselves (more on that later in the Bathroom), it is truly the room where we reveal what we believe is safe. After all, we don't allow ourselves to become this vulnerable around people and things that are threats.

Nakedness is trust. It reveals what we believe will be the greatest blessing to our most vulnerable selves.

This raises an ultimate question: What and who are you willing to be naked with, and why?

This isn't just a matter of clothing; it's a matter of honesty, humility, and dependence.

And while we've spent some time discussing sex and the byproducts of certain sexual choices, the idea of "nakedness" is hardly reserved to this spicy conversation topic.

Have you ever been "nakedly" honest?

Have you ever admitted "naked" fear?

Have you ever revealed your heart, exposing the "naked" truth?

Here's the reality: We only expose our true selves in situations where we feel that we're about to be met in the most intimate way.

That boils down to a stark choice between trusting in God to love you and provide for you, versus trusting in the world or your own self-determination.

Yes, you may physically "get naked" with someone on a regular basis, and whether you should or shouldn't is a different matter entirely. Do you get that intimate with God? Do you bare your most precious desires, insecurities, and worries with Him like this? Do you trust that He can satisfy your urgings and cravings more than any other?

Or do you regularly depend on yourself and the cheap, momentary remedies offered by the world?

Let me put this contrast another way, posing them as opposing activities in the bedroom:

- Wake up and stare at your phone for 30 minutes vs. Wake up, read some Scripture, spend 30 minutes in prayer

- Take a nap vs. Kneel or bow and reflect on what the Lord has done for you

- Binge-watch TV in bed vs. Read a devotional before sleeping

- Pray for patience and purity vs. Indulge in sexual gratification outside of marriage

Choosing to be so consistently intimate with the Lord is diametrically opposed to what the world tells us will make us happy. Being still and quiet doesn't sell; instead, we're urged to watch the next episode, then the next, and the next. We're told, *You deserve a break,* and told that all sorts of things will make us feel better, when the one thing we *really* need is intimate time with our Creator.

I'm not trying to make you feel bad for watching your favorite show or catching a cat nap in between activities. Don't be like the Pharisees, or the Puritanical person who demands perfect purity from everyone.

Rather, this is about where you believe your ultimate provision comes from.

And yes, that includes sex.

Do you believe God really cares for you, and wants to provide for you abundantly and generously?

Or do you fear that He's holding back, leaving you to fend for yourself?

This is exactly what Satan asked Eve in the garden. "'Did God *really say* you must not eat the fruit from any of the trees in the garden?' he asked the woman," (Genesis 3:1, emphasis added).

This question is at the heart of every temptation to withhold our naked passions from God. Will God *really* take care of me? Can I *really* trust Him to renovate this room of my life into something good and delightful? Or is He holding something back, like a cruel parent or unjust teacher?

Preparing for Marriage

Maybe for you, the bedroom has been this delicate space, this room where your self-worth has been tested, shattered, or misshapen. Maybe, like me, it became the room where you first questioned if you were lovable at all.

This brings me to a very personal story. One that shaped how I viewed myself, how I saw relationships, and how I understood intimacy—both the broken version and the holy kind.

When I approached the age of 40 and decided to get married, it was a time filled with excitement and uncertainty. I had lived a full life as a single woman—traveling, growing in my faith, building ministry, and enjoying a deeply personal relationship with God. But nothing could have prepared me for the subtle wave of fear that met me once I said, "I do."

You see, I was able to find peace in my Single Bedroom.

Perhaps this is because I didn't get married until my late thirties, and I had several years to work out my intimacy issues and transform the Bedroom into a wonderfully sacred space. It was the place I had learned to meet with God, a sanctuary where I could be unguarded, where I prayed, wept, listened, and rested in the Lord's presence.

That room held years of my intimacy—not with a man, but with the Holy Spirit. To share it now, even with someone I loved and respected, felt like handing over the key to a deeply private chamber of my soul.

I still remember the night I realized I was going to marry Rodney. We had been dating for a while—jogging together, serving in ministry, cheering on the Dallas Cowboys, just genuinely enjoying life side by side. One evening, I sat on the edge of my bed in quiet meditation when a sudden wave of emotion hit me. I began to cry out, "Lord, I don't want to leave You!"

I wasn't trying to be dramatic. I wasn't even trying to be spiritual. I was just being honest.

In that moment, I realized I was afraid of something wholly unexpected. It wasn't the fear of losing freedom or commitment.

It was the fear of losing the time, space, and depth I had cultivated with Jesus in my solitude.

As the night went on and the tears kept coming, I wept, "No, I don't want to leave You." And somewhere in the early morning hours, a whisper came: *"He will not make you choose."*

That was the moment everything shifted.

It was no longer about giving up something sacred. It was about expanding it.

This wasn't about replacing my relationship with God—it was about inviting Rodney into that sacred space and trusting that God could still be at the center.

The Apostle Paul speaks to this tension in 1 Corinthians 7:32-35: "I want you to be free from the concerns of this life. A woman who is no longer married or has never been married can be devoted to the Lord and holy in body and in spirit. But a married woman has to think about her earthly responsibilities and how to please her husband. I am saying this for your benefit, not to place restrictions on you. I want you to do whatever will help you serve the Lord best, with as few distractions as possible," (1 Corinthians 7: 32, 34–35).

I had enjoyed the gift of singleness. I was thriving in it. So much so that the idea of marriage felt disruptive. I even thought, "Well then, I don't want to ever get married."

Funny enough, Rodney hadn't said anything about marriage yet! I was over here wrestling with angels about a proposal that hadn't even been made.

But then came another moment that I'll never forget.

Rodney and I were driving to his house in Spartanburg, SC, to pick something up before a long training run. As he drove, I stared out the passenger window, lost in thought. Suddenly, tears started falling.

Rodney gently placed his hand on my shoulder and asked, "Nat, what's wrong?"

Without thinking, I whispered, "I don't want to leave Him to be with you."

I know—what a thing to say to your man! I could feel the atmosphere shift, and I worried I'd just nuked my chances with someone I had already fallen deeply in love with.

But to his credit, Rodney didn't flinch as I went on sharing everything—my night of weeping, the fear of losing my sacred time, the encounter that shook me to my core. He listened with grace.

A few days passed. Then, during a casual conversation, Rodney looked at me and said, "I'm not going to take you from God. I don't want your attention to be divided. Keep doing what you're doing—we'll plan everything else around that."

In that moment, I knew he saw me. He saw the depth of my relationship with God and didn't feel threatened by it. That was when I knew we could build a life together—not by replacing the sacred, but by building a new sacred space, one that made room for *us* while keeping Jesus at the center.

The bedroom would never be the same—and that was a good thing.

Let Him Provide

If the bedroom is where we are truly our most vulnerable self, it would be to our great benefit to guard it as if our lives depended on it.

To pray for its sanctity and protection. To beg Jesus to post angels around it and keep Satan out at all costs. To appoint it as a haven for beautiful unions—between us and Jesus, and someday between us and a spouse.

Remember that where the bedroom is wrong, the whole house is wrong. Let Margaret Kennedy's wise words serve as a daily call to arms, rousing us to fight on our knees in prayer that we don't fall victim to Satan's lies and allow him to usher shame into the spaces of intimacy.

God is your provider, especially in the Bedroom. He doesn't just give us food, clothing and shelter, but companionship, intimacy, and holy vulnerability. He is trustworthy and good in these things, even when the world tries to frighten us with loneliness and sell us broken solutions.

Let's do all we can to surrender the Bedroom to the Lord so that He can renovate it into the place of rest and restoration we need it to be.

Reflection Questions

1. What emotions does the word *bedroom* stir in you—peace, shame, joy, fear?

2. Have you ever experienced trauma, grief, or betrayal in your personal spaces? How have you processed that?

3. What does intimacy with God look like in your life right now? How has that relationship shaped your understanding of intimacy with others?

Journaling Prompt

What lies about intimacy have you believed in the past that God is now correcting? How is He redefining love, connection, or worth for you?

My Prayer for You

Father,

Thank you that you are with us in our most vulnerable spaces, especially the bedroom. Lord, there will be times when we fail to trust You, wait for You, and rely on Your provision. Please forgive us when we give into temptation and rush to satisfy our own desires with solutions that don't flow from You. Please give us patience to wait on You and trust in Your bountiful, generous gifts for us.

I pray for those who are struggling with boundaries, that You would guide them in establishing healthy, godly limits in their relationships. Give them the wisdom to know who is worthy of entering this sacred space of their hearts and the courage to guard it with integrity and grace.

For anyone feeling lonely or unseen, I ask that You would remind them of Your constant presence. May they experience Your nearness in the quiet moments, even when the world feels distant. Let them know that intimacy with You is never out of reach, no matter the season they are in.

Finally, may those who feel hopeless find their hope not in another human being's presence, but in Yours; we know You are faithful and work Your will in mysterious, beautiful ways that don't always make sense to us. Give us patience and perseverance so that we never fall out of love with You, even when we are weak and weary.

In Jesus' Name, Amen

Married Bedroom

The Room of Fire and Intimacy

"You are altogether beautiful, my darling; there is no flaw in you." —Song of Solomon 4:7 (NIV)

The first few weeks of my marriage weren't what I thought they would be. Yes, Rodney and I began to grow together in all the ways one might expect a pair of newlyweds to do so.

But something for me was off. It showed up whenever I was about to enter the bedroom.

Once we married, I moved into Rodney's house. While I was familiar and comfortable with the space, in my mind it was still his.

That's why I did something strange whenever I approached the bedroom door: I knocked.

Further, I kept calling it *his* bedroom. That's what it had been throughout the time we dated, after all!

This "imposter" mindset didn't stop there. I refused to use the *en suite* shared bathroom; that, too, had been exclusively his. Instead I'd tiptoe to the guest restroom down the hall, quietly closing the door behind me like a respectful visitor. Even in the middle of the night while Rodney soundly slept, I'd make off down the hall as if I was a prowler up to no good.

For some reason, I couldn't find comfort with the idea that this room was now "mine." I didn't even keep most of my clothes there. Every morning I'd sneak into the guest room and use its closet and bathroom to get ready—even after my husband had left for work. If he was still asleep, I'd sneak back to "our" room like nothing ever happened.

This carried on for months. Legally and spiritually I was Rodney's wife; mentally and emotionally, I was a guest overstaying her welcome.

Finally, Rodney seemed to notice and decided to say something. "Natalie?" he gently asked. "Why are you knocking on the door before coming into the bedroom?"

My secret was out. He'd noticed, and now I was going to have to own whatever this was.

"I guess I'm having trouble accepting that your bedroom is now *our* bedroom."

He was gracious, as always. "Of course it's ours, together. We're married, Natalie!"

For years, I had enjoyed the sanctity of my own private space. While I loved Rodney and was eager to join my life to his, I wasn't ready yet to hand it all over. I wasn't ready for the *real* cost of intimacy.

And to be fair, I wasn't confident about what it would mean to disrupt his sanctity, either. Just as the self-reliance of my singleness was about to be refined in the fires of marriage, so were his.

For that is what marriage really is: A purifying fire, a journey of raw, intimate sanctification meant to bring you ever closer to Jesus.

Your spouse isn't your savior. Your spouse isn't your god.

But when you choose to get married, you agree to let your spouse act as God's primary method of sanctifying you.

The Two Fires

The married bedroom often plays two divergent roles: The honeymoon suite, and the war zone.

Both burn with passion, but one consumes while the other purifies.

The world has sold us a fictitious picture of marriage. Thanks to Disney princesses, Danielle Steele romances, and other kinds of illicit smut, we often grow up believing that marriage will satisfy all our longings and fill every emptiness.

Lonely? Get married.

Hormonal? Get hitched.

Aimless and purposeless? Find a partner.

Yet the chief aim of marriage is not about pleasure, but purification; God's goal with His holy institution is not sex or satisfaction, but sanctification.

Yes, God gave us numerous forms of physical intimacy to enrich and amplify the beauty of marriage. Through this blessed covenant, we can transform once-sinful urges and longings and make them perfect again. Sex and intimacy can heal, soothe, and rebuild what was broken. And perhaps best of all, this is God's intended path toward reproduction, giving us the gift of new life!

But sex and pleasure are far from the main purposes of marriage, and this misalignment of expectations is one of the primary drivers of dissatisfaction and conflict in our relationships.

That's why it doesn't take long for the bedroom to transform from a paradise into a prison. No longer are you cuddling up with your lover, but trapped in a small space with someone who seems to bring out the worst in you.

This is where marriage *really* begins.

Any two consenting adults can have sex.

But can any two consenting adults forgive, reconcile, and rebuild what is broken, over and over again through every kind of trial and hardship?

Not at all.

That's why the Married Bedroom must be protected at all costs. It's why you cannot keep knocking on *his* or *her* door, fleeing to the guest bathroom, or keeping your clothes in a separate closet. You must embrace the awkward vulnerability of marriage, the embarrassing, cringe-worthy intimacy, and decide that you will love this person no matter what.

That doesn't just mean pledging to love them *if* they don't deserve it, or *if* they're unlovable.

It means committing to love them *when* these things happen, because they will. They'll happen for you and they'll happen for your spouse.

And that's the entire goal of marriage.

Marriage and the Gospel

A pastor and friend of mine once said, "All dating is posing."

When we fall in love, pursuing and courting a potential mate, we strive to win them over. We perform at our best. We exert ourselves to cover any flaws, mistakes, or errors. We dress up our pasts to make them as nonoffending as possible.

But in marriage, this performance quickly falls apart. The fiery intimacy of the Married Bedroom has a tendency to expose our true selves, and what we often find is never as attractive or appealing as what we offered during dating.

This may seem like a flaw, but I want to argue that it is a feature—at least of Biblical marriage.

Marriage wasn't created so we can be on our best behavior. Rather, marriage is one of God's primary tools for revealing our brokenness, and then sanctifying it according to His will.

In Ephesians, Paul describes how the Gospel *really* works, and marriage is no different: "Salvation is not a reward for the good things we have done, so none of us can boast about it," he states. "For we are God's masterpiece. He has created us anew in Christ Jesus, so we can do the good things he planned for us long ago," (Ephesians 2:9-10).

The goal of marriage isn't a perfect performance; it's perfect grace.

The world tells us to be perfect, and we gladly accept the challenge. We dress up our public appearance; we defend our reputations; we put our good works on display; we tell the truth only when it upholds our causes.

Yet Christ's teachings give us demonstrably opposite commands: Be humble; don't defend yourself; keep your generosity hidden; tell the truth, even if it makes you look terrible.

The gospel is not about our perfection, but constant repentance and trust in Jesus Christ. We have no hope in our own performance; yet when we depend entirely on the goodness of Jesus, His Spirit fuels us to do unimaginably wonderful deeds in our lives.

Marriage is no different.

We've been deceived into thinking that love in relationships is about how loveable we are, and our partners are.

But real marital harmony comes from the one True Love, Jesus Christ Himself.

If you aren't loving your spouse to Christ, and through Christ, then you're not *really* loving them at all.

You might be *enjoying* them, *using* them, or *tolerating* them.

But you're not loving them with the love that Christ gave to the church when He lived, died, and rose again on our behalf.

You Can't Love Enough

We're obsessed with the idea of love.

It's the topic of our favorite songs; the plot of our favorite movies. It's the drive of our lives.

Yet love fades. It changes. More than anything else, it slowly fades like the last embers of a once-roaring fire.

I don't mean to be negative or overdramatic; ask any couple that's been together for 10 or more years and you'll hear the truth. Love alone isn't enough. You need more if your marriage is going to endure.

Thankfully God knows this about us and is hard at work to supply us with all the love we need. But this isn't worldly love. It's not love of self, love of comfort, or love of pleasure.

The only "love" that can keep your marriage burning bright is the sacrificial love of Jesus.

When giving advice to husbands and wives, Paul has this advice for the guys: "...Love your wives, just as Christ loved the church. He gave up his life for her to make her holy and clean, washed by the cleansing of God's word," (Ephesians 5:25-26).

Notice that Paul doesn't say "love her passionately" or "try to stay attracted only to her." Paul uses the ultimate source of Love itself, God in the flesh, as the standard. And what action does Paul identify as the truest expression of love? Giving up one's life. This doesn't necessarily mean dying for one's wife, at least in the most dramatic sense. It means giving up the things one sees as life-bringing: Comforts, preferences, privileges.

As Jesus explains in Matthew 16, "'If you try to hang on to your life, you will lose it. But if you give up your life for my sake, you will save it,'" (Matthew 16:25).

You can't possibly love your spouse enough to keep your marriage strong. As a thing of clay, a mortal human being, you are simply not strong enough. I'm not strong enough, and neither is Rodney.

But Jesus is, and it's by following His example of sacrificial love that we find the power to keep the flame of marriage burning hot and strong, even in the harsh, bitter cold of life's trials.

When Trauma Comes After "I Do"

For some, marriage isn't just hard, but devastating.

For some, the bedroom has never been a place of rest—it has been a room of trauma, betrayal, and fear. The same room that should offer security and warmth can become a place of violation or torment.

And because of that, some people avoid being alone with themselves or in their thoughts, even in their own bed. They keep the lights on. TVs running. Doors cracked open.

Because silence sometimes shouts too loud. It whispers threats that trigger memories in the mind and the body.

Worse, some bedrooms become crime scenes, places of unspeakable hurts committed within the supposed sanctity of the marriage promise.

The Bible does not shy away from the reality that not every bedroom story is beautiful. Some of the most haunting events in Scripture took place behind closed doors.

In 2 Samuel 4:7, two men crept into Ish-Bosheth's bedroom while he was lying on his bed. They killed him in his sleep—a brutal act of betrayal in what should have been the safest space. In Judges 16, Delilah, in the privacy of Samson's bedroom, coaxes him into revealing the secret of his strength. What began as intimacy ended in deception and capture. The room meant for connection became a trap.

Then there's the deeply painful story of Tamar in 2 Samuel 13:10. Her own brother lured her into a private space under the guise of care and violated her there. The bedroom became a place of devastation and injustice.

Satan thrives on striking us when we are most vulnerable; this is often in the times and spaces where we expect to be fully protected.

And why not? Shouldn't a wife trust that her husband will put her safety and comfort first? Shouldn't a husband believe that his wife will honor him, remain loyal to him, and lift him up?

At our best—when we are fully dependent on the Spirit—this may be our experience in marriage.

But we are usually not at our best, and therefore our marriages tend to be riddled with unhealed wounds.

What happens, then, to these wounds?

They fester, seep, and spread. They grow into bitter tumors that kill the marriage from the inside out, insidious monsters chewing through our One Flesh until it is practically dead.

For this is Satan's second strategy: After poisoning a marriage with wounds, to totally destroy it with silence, leaving the infection to spread into all-out resentment.

This is why couples wake up in their tenth or fifteenth or twentieth year, look over at their spouse, and feel like they're in bed with a total stranger. This is why people who used to talk for hours, endlessly entranced with one another's dreams, struggle to utter a single sentence. This is why so many unions crumble once the kids move out.

For the strength of a marriage isn't based on how long it lasts; people will endure all sorts of suffering, so long as it is familiar and non-fatal.

But once the artificial reasons to stay together are gone—the kids, the mortgage, the business, the great sex—the partnership dissolves since it was never really there to begin with.

This is why a marriage must be founded on Christ, and Christ alone. He is the one thing that endures all of life's changes. He is the one love that can triumph over the myriad evils of Satan.

And He is the only one who can transform your Marriage Bedroom into a more beautiful reflection on His covenant with the church.

So if your marriage isn't built on this one true foundation, it's time to ask yourself: What *is* it built on, and how long do we have before it's gone?

Reclaiming the Married Bedroom

The process of healing a wounded marriage and rebuilding it on the solid rock of Jesus Christ is a lengthy, complicated process. This book and chapter can't accomplish that, as much as I'd love to do so.

Thankfully we live in a day and age where seeking therapy is applauded. Even if your marriage seems "fine," consider an enrichment or strengthening course. Just as you must invest in your physical health and finances, your marriage needs ongoing upkeep and maintenance. This is not a bad thing; it's just not what you're going to see in mainstream portrayals of marriage. It's not the societal "norm," at least not yet.

The first and most powerful step in renovating and reclaiming your Marriage Bedroom is to talk about what's happening in it.

This undermines one of Satan's tactics—silence—and gets things out in the open.

Because we tend to suffer in our minds. We bottle up our griefs and hold them close, fearful of how others will react.

Counseling forces brief, momentary discomfort but leverages it to create lasting, enduring peace.

Therapy also helps redefine the idea of "happiness" or "success" in a marriage, shifting our expectation away from simple comfort and toward constant sanctifying growth.

By default, we hate sanctification. It hurts. Our present goals, dreams, and desires must be put to death—or at least be set aside for a long period of time—in favor of a higher, more disciplined calling.

Sanctification is literally being "set apart" by God for holiness, and since marriage is one of God's primary vehicles for this divine work, we must come to expect it to be a regular part of how things go with our spouses.

A mature marriage isn't one with no conflict or issues; it's one where husband and wife actively engage in the process of communication, awareness, repentance, and reconciliation. A healthy marriage isn't one where neither spouse ever hurts the other; it's a relationship where both members realize, 'I'm *constantly* hurting the other, and only God can make me better.'

That's what it means to build your marriage on the foundation of Christ and His Gospel: Believe that you are a sinner in need of daily grace, and transparently commit yourself to that process.

Choose Your Fire

The marriage bedroom can be one of two fires: The fire of passion, or the fire of war.

Only you can choose which.

There is no alternative. There is no "pause" button on a relationship. Intimacy between partners is like a pair of powerful magnets: Either you are anxiously pulling together, or violently repelling one another.

If you truly feel that your marriage is not either of these fires, and it is nothing more than embers and ash, don't fall victim to the lie that your union is beyond saving. The Lord brought fire on the mountain for Elijah, and He can bring it into your marriage.

The key is to do the hard work: The communication and sanctification. The repentance and reconciliation.

Choosing marriage is choosing the intense heat and intimacy. That heat can keep you alive amid the snows of winter, and it can scar you and bring you near to death. Marriage is no mere partnership or hook up. It's a battle of the most important kind.

Whenever the heat in your relationship becomes too volcanic, and you feel like your spouse has become your worst mortal enemy, run to Christ. Run to the one who shows us the way: His life, His death, and His redemptive work.

Only in Jesus can we see what it is to love one's enemy, and to pray for those who persecute us. Only in Christ can we bring life to that which is dead.

I know that not all marriages can or even should be saved; some have been ravaged by abuse, relentless unfaithfulness, or verbal and emotional cruelty.

But your covenant is worth the effort. The Bedroom is worth entering boldly, without fear or any sense of impostership, and claiming as your own.

This is all a foretaste of the all-satisfying joy of heaven to come; yet we must struggle for it, working out our faith with fear and trembling, both in the Married Bedroom and out of it. And we must constantly give this room back to the Lord, as He is the creator of it. It is only God that can renovate and restore this sacred space for His glory and our good.

No marriage is perfect. But He is, and He gives us everything we need to bring beauty into every broken bit of the union He is building between us and our beloved.

Reflection Questions

1. The chief aim of marriage is not about pleasure, but purification; God's goal with His holy institution is not sex or satisfaction, but sanctification. How does this perspective challenge or affirm your own understanding of marriage and its purpose?

2. Paul advises husbands to "love your wives, just as Christ loved the church. He gave up his life for her." In what practical ways can you "give up your life" for your spouse, prioritizing their well-being and growth over your own comforts or preferences?

3. The first and most powerful step in reclaiming a wounded marriage is to talk about what's happening in it. What steps can you take, either individually or with your spouse, to initiate or deepen honest communication about the challenges and aspirations within your marriage?

Journaling Prompt

The chapter describes an "imposter mindset" in the early weeks of marriage. In what ways have you experienced a similar feeling of not fully belonging in or "owning" your shared life or spaces within your marriage?

My Prayer for You

Father,
I lift up every person who has walked through this chapter, and I thank You for the sacred space You've created within their hearts—the bedroom of their soul. I pray that You would help them see this room not only as a place of vulnerability but as a place where true intimacy with You and others can flourish.

Lord, for those who may feel fear or discomfort at the thought of sharing their innermost selves, I ask that You bring healing to any wounds that have been caused by broken trust or unmet needs. Surround them with Your love and peace, reminding them that they are fully known and fully loved by You. Help them know, Lord, that they are enough just as they are in Your eyes.

Lord, I ask for Your restoration in the bedrooms of their lives—whether it be for healing from broken relationships, trust restored, or new rhythms of connection in marriage. May their hearts be open to the work You want to do in them, and may they surrender the parts of themselves they've kept hidden, trusting You to bring renewal.

Finally, Lord, I pray that the bedroom of the soul would remain a place of rest in Your presence, a place where they encounter Your peace, Your love, and Your transforming power. As they move forward in their relationships—whether with You, a spouse, or others—may they do so with the confidence that they are first and foremost Your beloved, created for deep intimacy with You.

In Jesus' Name, Amen

Bathroom

The Room of Release and Refreshment

> *"But if we confess our sins to him, he is faithful and just to forgive us our sins and to cleanse us from all wickedness."*
> —1 John 1:9

One late night, I found myself in the restroom, leaning against the wall against the towel rack with a heart full of questions and concerns. I felt isolated—not from people, but from God.

Despite knowing deep down that He would never leave or forsake me, my mind couldn't grasp this truth. Weeks had passed like this. It was so overwhelming that I found myself yelling, "Where are you? Why haven't you come to see about me?"

This was one of the few times in my life, amidst all the ups and downs, that I felt abandonment creeping up on me. It was something that I had never experienced to this magnitude before. I began questioning everything—had I done something to displease God? Was I in a state of sin, blocking my access to Him?

What was *really* happening?

After a few hours of torment in these thoughts, I decided to go to bed, knowing I had a lot ahead of me the next day. I washed my face, tied up my hair, turned off the bathroom light, and as I stepped away, I whispered, "Lord, help me. Do you hear me? Help me."

This was around 1:00 AM.

Later that night, or should I say early that morning well before sunrise, a loud *bang!* jolted me awake. I opened my eyes to see flashing lights outside my window. The banging hammered again, thundering against my front door.

Heart pounding, I peeked out the blinds to see an ambulance and police car in the parking lot right in front of my apartment.

I crept to the door, trembling. "Who is it?"

Outside, a man's voice loudly asked, "Natalie, are you okay?"

I was baffled. *How did he know my name?*

Maybe there had been an emergency in another unit. "I don't understand," I said.

But he asked again, "Natalie, are you okay?"

"Yes, yes I'm fine!" I answered.

"Ma'am, we need you to open the door to prove you're safe."

That made no sense. Why *wouldn't* I be fine?

But I complied, opened the door, and saw two men standing there in uniform.

"We received a 9-1-1 call to render aid to this location, to you," they explained. "Are you sure everything is alright?"

"Yes, everything is fine," I said. "No one called from here. I was asleep."

"Well, we were alerted to a potential emergency at this location," they assured me.

Perplexed, I checked my phone. Had I dialed 9-1-1 in my sleep?

There was nothing. No calls since the middle of the day yesterday.

They asked to confirm my name and address via my license, and I gladly showed them. This merely confused us all the more.

As they departed, I tried to convince myself it was a mistake. Surely someone had given the wrong name or an errant address.

But I couldn't find peace with that explanation—they literally had my exact name *and* address.

The next day, I felt like I was in a daze, constantly wondering, "What was that all about?"

So I went to the local fire station; I needed to confirm they had actually been to my town home and that the whole thing wasn't just a wildly lucid dream.

Yet no one could verify the visit.

What?

I felt dizzy. The whole thing was increasingly bizarre. I shared the experience with a few people, but had no proof that the pre-dawn visit ever happened at all.

But then, a twist: As I pulled up to my home that evening after work, a neighbor was standing outside, waiting for me.

"Is everything okay, Natalie?" she asked. "I saw an ambulance and police here the other night."

You'd think I was on trial for murder or something, and this lady was a credible witness that could get me off! Thankfully, I had some proof that this moment really did happen.

Reflecting on that night, I remembered the last thing I said to God before going to bed: "God, help me!" Well, that's exactly what He did. He sent help to come check on me in a way I had never experienced, and I am sure that I will never experience again. I was reminded of David's proclamation in Psalm 34: "I sought the Lord, and he answered me and delivered me from all my fears," (Psalm 34:4).

This encounter changed how I think about prayer and God's presence. It may sound strange, but believe me, it was even stranger to live through it. I'm not expecting anyone to have the same experience, but I know God answers prayers uttered in the metaphorical Bathroom—that private space where we retreat to be alone.

Unfortunately many of us do not make ourselves enough of a priority to have space to just breathe. To retreat. To shut out the noise of the world and make room for God's voice.

I want to encourage you right now that God is in your space of retreat, eager for consistent and constant connection with you. Those who make the decision to draw closer to Him always find that He in turn will draw closer to them.

I'll never forget the night where I cried out to God from my spirit and He answered me in an unexpected, tangible way. The release that happened in my physical Bathroom became a real experience that changed the way I think, feel and experience my place of surrender.

Let's take a moment to consider whether we've created a space for retreat and rejuvenation in our lives, where we go for our privacy, cleansing, and release, and where we go to find solace and connection with God.

How Greeks Did Their Business

Imagine a time around 3000 B.C.

Communal baths are mystical sanctuaries, more about spiritual cleansing than scrubbing away the dirt.

Fast forward to 1700 B.C. We find the first personal bathtubs in Crete, eerily similar to what we use today.

However, the fall of the Roman Empire marks a decline in bathing practices, with the Renaissance era bringing fears that water could carry diseases. People turned to sweat baths and heavy perfumes instead.

The real game-changer came in the 14th century when Edward I installed the first bathroom in the Palace of Westminster—a true innovation. King Henry VII later shut down public bathhouses in 1546, blaming them for the plague, further pushing the evolution of private bathing.

The 18th century saw the dawn of a new era. The wealthy installed taps and running water in their homes, making private bathing a luxurious reality. However, the Industrial Revolution kicked things up a notch, introducing hot water systems and gas heaters that brought the luxury of personal baths to the middle class.

Why did this matter so much?

In a word: Germs.

The discovery of microscopic bugs revolutionized how people thought about cleanliness, making regular bathing—and not just with steam or perfume, but with soap—a popular health trend.

By the 20th century, bathrooms had transformed into stylish, comfortable spaces integral to every home. This momentum continued in the 1960s, making bathrooms a common feature even in working-class domiciles. Today modern bathrooms are technological havens with underfloor heating, special ventilation, mood lighting, and every imaginable digital amenity, offering a personal retreat for relaxation and luxury.

It's amazing how a room in your house can truly become a sanctuary. For instance, after a long and stressful day, many people find solace in a warm bath filled with soothing essential oils like lavender or eucalyptus. This not only relaxes the muscles but also calms the mind, providing a much-needed break from daily stressors.

Or for many, the bathroom is where they start their day with a rejuvenating shower, wallowing in invigorating scents like citrus or peppermint to awaken the senses and prepare them for the day ahead.

It's a place to gather thoughts, set intentions, and step into the world feeling refreshed and confident. For parents the bathroom is often the only place where one can get a moment of peace and quiet, a quick escape to brush teeth or wash one's face. The Bathroom is a sacred place where one can capture a few precious minutes of silence to breathe and collect themselves before returning to life's many responsibilities.

The Bathroom, in all its simplicity, offers countless opportunities for renewal, reflection, and rejuvenation, making it an essential part of our daily lives.

So, too, is our ultimate place of retreat: The Presence of God. The question is whether you're taking advantage of all His promises, including those that ask you to cleanse and refresh your filthiest parts.

Girl, Wash Your Face

Countless films depict restrooms as sanctuaries where characters retreat to gather themselves.

Whether in a private bathroom at home or a bustling public restroom, these settings symbolize moments of intense introspection and self-confrontation.

- Picture the title hero of *Rocky* staring into the mirror, grappling with self-doubt before a big fight, the reflection not just of his face but his inner turmoil

- In *The Devil Wears Prada*, Andy splashes water on her face, seeking a moment of clarity amidst the whirlwind of her new job

- And in *Black Swan*, Nina's frequent trips to the restroom mirror her unraveling under pressure

These scenes tap into a universal human experience: The need to step away, look ourselves in the eye, and muster the strength to face what's ahead. These cinematic moments draw us in, making us feel the characters' struggles and triumphs as if they were our own.

The bathroom, as a room of retreat and transformation, becomes a powerful metaphor for life, reminding us that no matter how chaotic things may get, we should always have a space to pause, reflect, and gather the strength to face our challenges head-on.

Consider: Where is your place of retreat in your life?

Many of us haven't yet discovered this sanctuary of peace, and as a result, life's challenges can feel overwhelming. Without that space to pause and reflect, it becomes not only difficult to face life's trials but also to confront our own reflections—the "man in the mirror."

Finding that place of retreat is crucial for our well-being and resilience, allowing us to gather the strength to move forward with clarity and purpose.

But just as we need a physical space for retreat, we need a spiritual one too. In Psalm 91, verses 1-2, David proclaims, "Those who live in the shelter of the Most High will find rest in the shadow of the Almighty." Our spiritual retreat—the one true place where we can enjoy total release, refreshment, and restoration—must be in Jesus Christ.

But how do we access that? How do we step into this sanctuary in a practical sense, just as we would an actual bathroom with all our favorite amenities?

We must hand the renovation over to the one who is acquainted with, and not embarrassed by, the reality of our mess.

Upgrade Your Bathroom

I love a good bathroom renovation. Few rooms can become gross as quickly as a bathroom, so a stunning before-and-after sequence on a home improvement show always gets me.

But while this kind of transformation may bring renewal to your physical restroom, it won't do anything for your heart.

Just as you invest resources into a bathroom flip, you must devote the necessary time and energy into the establishment of your heart's "Bathroom," the place where you go to seek total cleansing and rejuvenation.

How do we do this?

It's not as easy to relax as we'd like. Many of my adult friends have shared that they don't know how to rest anymore, since life is filled with constant to-do lists, tasks, and responsibilities.

That's why I recommend using this 3-step process to ease into your Bathroom process and enjoy a full, complete restoration from the Holy Spirit:

1. Release your waste

2. Wash with the Word

3. Let Him refresh you

Let's briefly look at how to take part in each:

Release Your Waste

Going to the bathroom is a fact of life. For some it's disgusting and embarrassing; for others, it's an endless source of humor.
Whatever your perspective is, the fact doesn't change that all human beings need to remove waste from their bodies.
This isn't just a physical reality, but a spiritual one, too. When waste doesn't properly pass out of our bodies, it disrupts everything else and even causes excruciating pain.
Spiritual waste—sin, shame, guilt, doubt, fear, anxieties—are no different. These impediments to walking in the Truth clog up our minds and cause us to endlessly strive to redeem ourselves. We try to be perfect or make everyone around us perfect; we lust for control because we believe it's the only thing that can make us feel peace.

Yet there is never enough control to feel peace; the only True, lasting peace comes from trusting in the Father.

To release your spiritual waste, and begin your Bathroom cleanse, step into a space where you can think and talk freely about what is getting you down. Journal, monologue, meditate, or pray about your current worries.

Pour out your frustrations to God and don't hold back. Just as you need a physical bathroom to get everything out—and preferably in privacy so you can avoid judgment—you need a way to flush every unholy element out of your system.

Don't worry about what God thinks. He knows you have to use the bathroom, both physically and spiritually.

So let it out.

Wash With the Word

Soap is essential to clean our bodies. Without it, microscopic germs will continue to grow and thrive on our flesh, leading to infections and unsettling odors.

Our spirits desperately want washing as well. Christianity uses several "washing" images for good reason: It's what we need.

Paul uses a great metaphor to describe how a man should love his wife: "For husbands, this means love your wives, just as Christ loved the church. He gave up his life for her to make her holy and clean, washed by the cleansing of God's word," (Ephesians 5:25-26).

While this image is contextually specific to the marriage relationship, it shows us that the only thing that can truly clean us from within is God's Word. Since Jesus Himself was the Word Incarnate, we're blessed with an abundance of spiritual soap.

I recommend choosing Scriptures that speak to His constant presence, His unfailing love, His limitless mercy, and His overflowing provision, and posting them in your Bathroom. You can write on the mirror with soap; you can print and laminate pieces of paper. Heck, even a sticky-note with a thumbtack can be enough.

Don't assume that a quiet space alone is enough to wash your spirit and rid it of Satan's corrupting filth. You need the True Soap that comes from the loving Son of God, Jesus Christ.

So use it; it's free and available for anyone who asks for it.

Let Him Refresh You

Lastly, take time in your bathroom to rest in silence, allowing the Holy Spirit of God to refresh you.

This takes time. Quiet, silence, or ambient music. Maybe it's candles or complete darkness. A long shower or bath.

Perhaps it's just you sitting on the toilet, lid-closed, with your head bowed.

Treasure this time. Don't rush it. You can't know all that the Lord of Heaven and Earth can do with the time you surrender to Him, but you can believe it will be precious.

Lasting refreshment doesn't come from creams, oils, scrubs, or lotions. Yes, these physical remedies are a delight, and I enjoy my fair share of them! But nothing compares to the Spirit of the Living God making you clean and refreshing your body, mind, and spirit for what lies ahead.

I know this last part is somewhat vague, but that's because it's so personal. For me, it was leaning against the wall and crying out to the Lord until someone called 9-1-1 on my behalf. Hopefully your process won't involve law enforcement!

But know that it's crucial to make time for the Lord to move. We are so hurried in our culture. Our attention is so divided by notifications, emails, and 24-hour news.

Step out of the noise and lean into His presence. Invite the Lord to join you in your Bathroom so that you can know your release and refreshment have been blessed by His Holy Hand.

Refreshment That Never Fades

Psalm 91:1-2 declares, "Those who live in the shelter of the Most High will find rest in the shadow of the Almighty. This I declare about the LORD: He alone is my refuge, my place of safety; He is my God, and I trust him."

God calls us to cherish a personal and intimate relationship with Him, nurtured in the quiet moments of retreat and reflection. When we answer this call by creating our own sacred spaces, both physically and spiritually, we open the door to receive God's presence and His renewing peace.

God calls us to wash our spiritual hands and cleanse our hearts. Just as the bathroom holds some of our messiest secrets but is essential for us to be truly clean, our spiritual retreat is where we bring our mess before the Cross of Christ. Trust that He can make it disappear and sanctify us. Though it may sound crass, we can rejoice that our sin and waste can both be flushed away!

So, whether you are retreating to be heard, cleansed, or alone with God, this place of retreat is your sanctuary.

Aren't you glad that in this secret place, you have a God who keeps your deepest and darkest thoughts as "secrets"?

Remember that when we enter this metaphorical bathroom, we are not grooming ourselves for worldly success or approval. Rather, we submit to the will of God and allow Him to restore us into our sanctified selves. We don't retreat selfishly or in vanity, but in humility. We know that only He can make us beautiful and clean again, so we run to Him.

As Paul writes in Galatians 4:6, "And because we are his children, God has sent the Spirit of his Son into our hearts, prompting us to call out, 'Abba, Father.'"

Every parent knows their child has waste that must be washed away; parents change diapers for years, fully aware of their infant's needs.

Our God is no different. He longs to care for us, clean us, soothe our wounds, and renew us. He isn't eager to shame us for being dirty, or publicly humiliate us for any imperfection. He is a good Father, a loving parent, tender and compassionate. We can trust Him with our mess, no matter how repulsive we fear it may be.

So as you enhance and upgrade your physical lavatory, invite the Lord to renovate your Spiritual Bathroom, too. Commit to releasing your spiritual waste, washing with the Word, and seeking out the refreshment and cleansing that can only come from our Father in Heaven.

Reflection Questions

1. What areas of my life am I holding onto that I need to release? Am I clinging to past hurts, guilt, or unhealthy habits that are preventing me from moving forward?

2. What "waste" do I need to flush out of my life? Are there toxic relationships, negative thought patterns, or burdens I need to let go of?

3. Do I trust God's cleansing power, or am I trying to "clean" myself up on my own? How can I surrender more fully to His grace and forgiveness?

Journaling Prompt

Who or what am I allowing to "dirty" my spiritual walk? What influences or distractions are keeping me from walking in purity and purpose?

My Prayer for You

Father,

Thank You for meeting us in the hidden places—those quiet rooms where we finally exhale, let go, and allow our hearts to be honest before You. For the one reading this prayer, I lift up their moments of exhaustion, their whispered questions, and the tears they have shed behind closed doors. You see everyone, and not a single drop is wasted in Your sight.

Lord, I pray this sacred "bathroom" space becomes a place of cleansing and renewal for them. Wash away the heaviness they have carried. Cleanse shame that clings like residue from battles long passed. Rinse fear from the corners of their mind, and let Your truth run over them like living water. Remove guilt that isn't from You, and refresh their spirit with Your loving presence.

Where they feel alone, remind them that You draw near to the brokenhearted. Where they feel dry, pour out new strength. Where they have been afraid to ask for help, give them courage to cry out to You again—knowing You respond, knowing You care, and knowing You show up even in the quiet moments where we least expect it.

Let the bathroom of their soul be a sanctuary of release and relief. May they find peace as they breathe in Your grace and breathe out every burden. May cleansing come not only to their emotions, but to their identity—restoring them to the truth that they are loved, treasured, and held safe in Your hands.

Father, meet them in the stillness. Renew their hope.

Refresh their mind. Restore their spirit.

In Jesus' name, Amen

OFFICE

THE ROOM OF OBLIGATIONS AND ENTICEMENTS

> *"Don't copy the behavior and customs of this world, but let God transform you into a new person by changing the way you think. Then you will learn to know God's will for you, which is good and pleasing and perfect."* —Romans 12:2

When my Aunt Willie got the phone bill and saw the word "Roaming" all over it, she was ready to kill me. My dorm room phone rang and I picked it up to the sound of her frantic voice: "Where are you? Who are you with?"

"I'm in my room," I said, perplexed. "What's the matter?"

"Tell me the truth, Natalie!" she exclaimed. "What are you doing? Don't make me come to that school!"

After several minutes of calming her down, I finally realized what had Aunt Willie so worked up: She had thought the word "Roaming" meant I was cruising the streets instead of being in class! Of course that's *not* what it means. In the early days of mobile phones, "Roaming" was a term that meant the phone was outside the coverage area, and that extra charges were involved.

Aunt Willie was relieved, and promised to call me on my dorm room phone from now on since it wouldn't cost so much. Plus she was just glad I wasn't loose on the streets!

In fact, while we were talking, I picked up my mobile phone and saw that it was literally roaming *while I was in my dorm room*. Neither of us knew much about cellular phones at the time, but you better believe we figured it out quickly that we'd need to get me a new plan! It was either that or not having a phone at all.

This experience makes me think about how, just like a mobile device, our minds often "roam" too. We can be physically present at work or in the Office, but our thoughts are wandering far beyond what's in front of us.

Just as my phone roamed outside its coverage area, our thoughts can roam without clear direction, carrying us to places that might not serve us in the moment.

We might find ourselves caught up in endless distractions, unresolved emotions, or even old patterns of thinking—leaving us disconnected from the present and our true purpose. And when that happens, we find ourselves falling short of the great works which the Lord has anointed for our joy and His glory.

The Office of Our Minds

Not all homes have a designated office, but that doesn't mean work doesn't happen in the home. Many professionals work from home, using a guest bedroom, closet, or alcove as the "Office." For families working to break through and move upward, one end of the dining room table might have to be enough.

Whether or not your home has its own proper office, it has a space where you find yourself fulfilling the obligations of keeping your home's affairs in order. That may be through an all-encompassing full-time remote job or a long struggle to balance the checkbook.

No matter how "The Office" manifests in your home, it does, and it reflects the way we answer God's call to use our gifts and talents to glorify him.

Offices have undergone a remarkable evolution since its inception in the pre-20th century. Once a space distinctly separated from home life, whether nestled within the confines of a three-walled cubicle or perched atop the skyscrapers of our great cities, the office has continuously transformed to meet the needs of the workforce. As the years rolled on, the office space shifted from towering skyscrapers to factory-like layouts, then to irregular geometric designs with potted plants and curved screens behind dividers. The emergence of laptops and the phrase "You've got mail" heralded a new era, making work portable and reshaping traditional office environments.

However, the advent of the internet—and then the boundary-breaking revolution of smartphone technology—made it possible for the office to no longer be a separate space. Now it's with us wherever we go, often to the detriment of our mental health and work-life balance.

Never was this more apparent than in 2020 when the world witnessed the greatest workplace experiment of all time, as a global pandemic forced countless professionals to transition from corporate offices to home offices. This shift brought about a profound change. Once upon a time, executives sat like kings in palatial offices, gate-kept by secretaries and schedules. By April of that year, we were seeing them through grainy webcams, desperately shooing their toddlers out the door or standing up, only to reveal themselves wearing pajama pants or boxer shorts.

This is why the Office isn't just a space in the house or workplace; it's a mindset, an attitude, and a belief about the role work plays in our walk with Jesus.

And in the Office of the mind, it's easy to act like we're still in the pandemic, showing up with only half of our outfit, or even hesitant to clock a full day. It's a space that easily becomes cluttered as we wrestle with the innumerable tasks of life—work, family, decisions, and dreams. It is also a space where we are lured away from our obligations, and instead submit ourselves to all sorts of unproductive—even *destructive*—enticements.

When we don't tend to our Office, organize it, clean it, and pay it proper attention, these buried responsibilities and duties can come back to haunt us.

It's just like my old phone's roaming function: Sometimes our subconscious thoughts can run away with us. And when those thoughts roam, it can feel like we're not fully present in our own lives, leading to a constant sense of purposelessness and dread.

When the Office is a Mess

Our thoughts shape everything about us.

In Proverbs 4:23, Solomon advises us to "Guard your heart above all else, for it determines the course of your life."

And in Luke 6:45, Jesus instructs his audience, "A good person produces good things from the treasury of a good heart, and an evil person produces evil things from the treasury of an evil heart. What you say flows from what is in your heart."

The mind and the heart are one. To put it practically, the heart longs and the mind plots, both actively seeking an objective.

There is perhaps no more powerful force for good or evil in our lives than our own minds.

This is why it's essential that we seek to control our thoughts at all costs. "Fix your thoughts on what is true, and honorable, and right, and pure, and lovely, and admirable," Paul writes. "Think about things that are excellent and worthy of praise," (Philippians 4:8).

Undoubtedly this sounds delightful and pristine. Why wouldn't we constantly let good things flow through our minds?

In a word: Satan. That's why. He doesn't make this easy or particularly enjoyable.

That's why he is always about the business of distracting us; he's the master of holding up a shiny object, whispering "Look over here!" and enticing us with it.

Most of the time, I'll admit that my thoughts are a complete and utter mess. I'll admit that sometimes I fall into conversation about the latest gossip or bad news. Since my latest smartphone is always updating me about things, I'm fully aware of all the trouble and evil going on in the world.

I'm fraught with worry, too. I stress about bills, payments, and debt. I recently began flipping houses and some days I fear that I bit off way more than I can chew.

There are many other things we're tempted to stress about. For you, it might be your relationship or marriage. Your children. Grandbabies, and the future of this world they'll have to grow up in.

I struggle with judgment. Not just of others, but of myself. Anytime I see myself in the mirror, my thoughts instantly turn critical, unable or unwilling to see God's image in myself.

My mental office is, honestly, a disaster—and yours probably is, too.

This is why we must be intentional in managing our thoughts. Otherwise we will never succeed in tackling our numerous obligations which others depend on us for.

And while this isn't easy, it is completely doable. Jesus did it, and He taught his followers to do the same.

Better yet, we have His Spirit within us, dwelling in our hearts to refine and sanctify them. Jesus literally gave us a divine renovation agent to coexist with us at all times!

If anyone can take their thoughts captive and make them more holy, it's you and me, followers of the One True God.

Is it Time for You to Switch Plans?

The next time I visited home from college, Aunt Willie and I went to our cellular carrier and switched plans. This new plan gave me more coverage and fewer surprises. That meant no more "roaming" charges and heart attacks for my auntie!

In the same way, spiritual disciplines—prayer, meditation on God's Word, and taking time for reflection—help us to "upgrade" our minds. When we align our thoughts with God's truth and seek His guidance, we can bring order to the chaos of our subconscious and find clarity in the midst of distractions.

Just as a more thoughtful plan brings stability to a phone, leaning into God's presence stabilizes our hearts and minds, allowing us to navigate life with peace and purpose. When we bring our thoughts under His control, we stop roaming aimlessly and begin to walk in the coverage of His grace.

Think about the process of cleaning an office. The desk is covered with clutter: Envelopes, sticky notes, papers and notebooks, empty cups and cans, towering stacks of books, and—if you're like me—crumpled Reese's wrappers.

It's messy. Unpleasant. It takes longer than you'd like.

You also have to make hard decisions. What do you keep? What must be parted with? You can't keep everything. And even if you keep something, it doesn't necessarily need to stay visible or within reach.

Cleaning the Office of your mind is very similar, but requires you to sift through less tangible clutter: Thoughts, plans, worries, goals, concerns, to-do lists. Yet these scattered ideas quickly become distractions that prevent us from hearing clearly or making sound decisions. Just like in the workplace, our minds need a system to operate efficiently—a plan that gives us coverage, a path to clarity, and the ability to navigate through complex emotions and situations.

We've all been in situations where our thoughts start to *roam*—anxiety over a decision, worries about the future, regrets about the past. These roaming thoughts can pull us in a million directions, making it difficult to focus on what matters most.

Let me ask you: Do you need a better plan for your *mental* space? Do you need to "upgrade" your coverage so you spend less time roaming in your thoughts?

I know I did, and I often still do.

Yet this upgrade doesn't occur in a cell phone store, but in quiet, focused time with the Lord. It continues with renewing our minds, a process that doesn't happen by accident but through intentional action—just like switching to a better mobile plan. Paul's reminder in Romans 12:2 holds immense significance in this context. "Don't copy the behavior and customs of this world, but let God transform you into a new person by changing the way you think. Then you will learn to know God's will for you, which is good and pleasing and perfect," (Romans 12:2).

The call to not "copy the behavior and customs of this world" is essentially a challenge to break free from the noise of our subconscious and the pressures of external influences. The world, much like an office plagued with clutter and potential distractions, diverts our focus and tries to mold us into something we are not.

Renewal Brings Peace We All Need

How do we go about seeking this renewal?

Thankfully, Scripture gives us clear stepping stones to move away from the world and its toxic thought patterns, and lean into the peaceful ways of Jesus Christ.

Renewal begins by diving into God's Word, surrendering our thoughts to Him, and allowing Him to guide our decisions, we are transformed. Our office, or mind, is no longer a chaotic space filled with roaming thoughts; it becomes a well-organized, focused haven where we can truly hear from God and walk in His will.

When we renew our minds, we are also given the ability to *discern*—to see clearly the direction God wants us to take. Imagine sitting in an office with papers scattered everywhere, and then suddenly, a gentle hand guides you to sort through the chaos, creating order and clarity. That's what happens when we allow God to perform this redemptive work: The mess begins to fade and we gain insight into what is good, acceptable, and perfect according to His will. This renewal is an active process, one that requires us to choose focus over distraction and trust over anxiety.

Isaiah 26:3 further underscores the results of this kind of mental renewal: "You will keep in perfect peace all who trust in you, all whose thoughts are fixed on you!"

We also move forward in this redemption by seeking to *trust* God fully. When we do, we are no longer subject to the mental roaming that leads to confusion and disarray. The Office of the mind becomes a sanctuary of peace.

Peace in the Hebrew context (*shalom*) means completeness, wholeness, and the absence of chaos. Imagine walking into an office where everything is in its place, every task is organized, and there's no tension in the air. That is what God promises to those whose minds are fixed on Him! A steadfast mind, one that is focused on His truth and trust in His ability to lead, experiencing His perfect peace.

To take it a step further, our trust in God means we no longer rely on our own understanding or the fleeting solutions that the world offers.

The author of Proverbs urges his "son" to heed this foundational mindset: "Trust in the LORD with all your heart; do not depend on your own understanding. Seek his will in all you do, and he will show you which path to take," (Proverbs 3:5-6).

It takes supernatural courage to trust in God *and* mistrust our own minds. We live in our minds constantly and tend to rely on their guidance.

Yet the wise author of Proverbs exhorts us to do otherwise. By trusting God's wisdom over our own, we can enjoy heavenly clarity and steadiness in our thoughts.

In other words, God Himself will come and clean your office!

The chaos and distractions of the world may swirl outside, but in our minds there can be an unwavering peace that guides our decisions, conversations, and actions.

This peace, however, doesn't come automatically. Just as I had to actively upgrade my mobile phone plan to get better service, we must actively upgrade our spiritual practices to experience God's peace. It's a daily commitment—one where we choose to reset our minds through prayer, worship, meditation on Scripture, and surrendering our worries to Him. If we want the freedom to fulfill our obligations with peace and purpose, this is what we have to do.

Here are some practical ways to get that process going today.

How to Renovate Your Office

Our subconscious, much like an office, stores a vast array of thoughts, emotions, memories, and experiences, many of which are shaped by external influences or past wounds. If left unchecked, these unchecked thoughts can mislead us, taking us away from truth and into unhealthy patterns of behavior.

1. Tidy Up

The office metaphor becomes all the more powerful when we imagine our minds as a messy desk filled with clutter: Scattered papers, half-finished tasks, unopened emails, and sticky notes everywhere. This clutter can represent unresolved issues, past traumas, harmful influences, and habitual thought patterns that we haven't processed properly.

Just as an office filled with junk is inefficient and hard to navigate, our subconscious filled with unchecked, negative thoughts becomes a breeding ground for confusion, fear, and sin. If we let these negative thoughts run free, they can begin to shape our behavior. We may begin to rely on the false narrative that these thoughts feed us, like believing we are inadequate, unworthy of love, or trapped in cycles of guilt.

These are the areas where sin often takes root.

To prevent sin from working its way in too deep, tidy up your mental office by practicing deliberate surrender.

This means purposefully and methodically handing things over to God. Make lists of your goals, worries, to-do items, and responsibilities. Then pray over each, giving control and authority over them to the King of Kings.

As we keep our "desk" tidy and our thoughts aligned with God's truth, we reduce the risk of allowing harmful patterns of thinking to shape our actions.

2. Control Your Emotions

Our subconscious is a cavernous place where we store emotional responses to situations, especially those that have caused us pain, fear, or disappointment. Over time, these emotional responses become ingrained in us, and if we're not careful, they can evolve into sinful patterns.

For example, if we've been hurt in the past, we may subconsciously resort to bitterness, anger, or withdrawal as a defense mechanism. These reactions aren't aligned with God's truth—they are responses shaped by our subconscious.

These emotional responses make it difficult to truly "keep work at work." This is especially true when you begin to get your identity from your work performance. When you professionally fail, it's hard not to see it as a personal or general failure, too.

These negative thought patterns become bad habits, and are just as hard to break as smoking or biting one's fingernails. The longer we lean into these avoidant tendencies, the more they will shape how we respond to the world.

The Apostle Paul equips us for the challenge with his admonition: "Be not overcome of evil, but overcome evil with good," (Romans 12:21).

This Scripture speaks to the power of choosing the ways of the Spirit over default, sinful responses that can arise from our subconscious. Instead of lashing out or harbor bitterness, lean into God's character of love, forgiveness, and grace—even in the workplace and world of productivity.

By removing these old patterns and replacing them with a renewed perspective that comes from God's Word, we can begin to react to life's challenges in ways that better align with His will.

3. Stay Focused and Avoid Enticement

The office is a place where we face temptation. In a corporate setting, distractions can lead employees to lose focus, waste time, or even make unethical decisions.

In the office of our minds, temptations can come in the form of lust, pride, greed, or envy. These thoughts may not immediately lead to outward sin, but if left unimpeded, they slowly begin to shape our character and actions. Every one of us has sat at a desk and constantly been tempted to scroll through social media or waste time on distractions instead of focusing on work.

When we allow these enticements to linger in our subconscious, they grow and take root in our hearts. What starts as a fleeting thought or temptation can become a recurring pattern in our minds that we feed with more attention. When our minds are "roaming," we open ourselves up to thoughts that quickly lead to sinful behaviors. That's why it's critical to guard our minds, just as a well-organized and managed work environment is built to prevent distractions.

James, the brother of Christ, encourages us in his epistle to "humble yourselves before God. Resist the devil, and he will flee from you. Come close to God, and God will come close to you. Wash your hands, you sinners; purify your hearts, for your loyalty is divided between God and the world," (James 4:7-8).

Temptation is not something to take lightly. Instead, we are reminded to assume a battle posture and resist it. James tells us to "come close to God," which we do when we wash ourselves in the Word, spend time in prayer, fellowship with the saints, and serve "the least of these."

These physical behaviors of outward submission empower us to submit our minds to God as well. Our actions say "No" to the lies of the enemy and "Yes" to the truth of God.

It's all about taking control of our thoughts in the "office of our minds" and refusing to let temptation lead us into sin. Just as an employee can set boundaries to focus on their work, we too can set mental and spiritual boundaries to protect our minds from sin.

4. Don't Neglect Regular Cleanings

One of the most important practices in maintaining a well-functioning office is regular clean-up and organization. File your papers; pick up trash; organize files; dust, wipe, and sanitize.

When things are clean they can run smoothly; but when junk and filth are all about us, it's difficult to concentrate and maximize the effectiveness of the workspace.

The same applies to our subconscious. Just as we would organize papers and delete old files from our desktop to make room for new, productive work, we must periodically examine and cleanse our minds of unhealthy patterns, old wounds, and sinful thoughts. This again is where spiritual disciplines like prayer, fasting, confession, and repentance come in. These practices act like a clean-up crew for our subconscious mind, helping us stay aligned with God's truth.

David prays in Psalm 51, "Create in me a clean heart, O God. Renew a loyal spirit within me," (Psalm 51:10).

This prayer is one we can adopt when we realize our subconscious has become a trash-ridden mess. Just as an office may need a deep cleaning, we too need God to cleanse us from the negative influences we've allowed into our minds. This renewal of the spirit is not just a one-time prayer but an ongoing process in which we surrender our thoughts to God, asking for His help to keep our Office organized and focused on what truly matters.

Roam If You Want To... But I Wouldn't

The office brings us to an important crossroads. We must face the disarray of our thoughts, the roaming distractions, and the negative patterns that have taken root.

Then we must answer: Will we continue to let our minds wander, aimlessly picking up messages that don't align with truth? Or will we choose to make the difficult but necessary decision to clear the mental clutter and submit our thoughts to God?

This is a key moment of sacrifice. It's easy to let our minds stray into unhealthy spaces because, on some level, it feels familiar. Those thought patterns—resentment, fear, anxiety, or jealousy—are comforting in their predictability. They allow us to avoid the discomfort of confronting deeper issues in our hearts.

But when we lean into these thoughts, we miss out on the transformation that comes with submitting our minds to God's Word. We stay in a place of emotional stagnation, unable to move forward in the ways God intends for us.

That's the beauty of God's Word: It's His constant method of renovating us from within. The Word has the power to demo our darkness and completely transform the remaining space into His likeness.

Therefore, let us stop roaming. Our free will and hedonistic culture invite us to roam where we want to, indulging every curiosity and impulse.

But to do so is ruinous, like pouring out the garbage can on top of one's desk. We must choose to stop accepting the thoughts that come into our minds at face value and instead submit them to the authority of God's truth.

As I did when I realized that my phone plan needed adjustment, we all must make the choice to shift our thinking away from worldliness and toward Godliness. We cannot simply hope things will change—we must intentionally step forward and make a commitment to renew our minds.

This is where true transformation happens—when we actively choose to bring our thoughts into alignment with God's truth and allow Him to guide us into clarity. As we choose to stop roaming, as we choose to come into alignment with God's Word, we find that peace takes root in our minds. We no longer feel trapped in cycles of sin and negativity. We no longer experience slavery to sin and the prison of thoughts it imposes.

Instead, we breathe new air, free in the gospel with minds refreshed and liberated by the Spirit.

Only then can we truly find peace and purpose in the obligations that God has called us to.

No longer weighed down by mental clutter. No longer aimless, wandering, and lost. No longer bound by chains of worldly enticements.

Let us cling to the beautiful promise that God alone, through His Holy Spirit, can bring peace in our thoughts—to the Office of our spiritual house.

Reflection Questions

1. Have you ever noticed your thoughts "roaming" in a way that led to anxiety or unhealthy patterns? How did you redirect them?

2. Where in your life is it hardest to live out God's truth in challenging situations? How can you shift your subconscious toward His truth?

3. What steps can you take when anxiety or stress builds in your subconscious? How can you replace those thoughts with peace?

Journaling Prompt

What practices can you implement to maintain spiritual clarity in your mind daily?

My Prayer for You

Father,

I thank You for the time we've spent together in this chapter. I'm so grateful for the opportunity to walk through this space of the mind with each person reading these words. I lift up every one of them to You now, asking that You continue to guide and strengthen them as they reflect on the truths we've explored together.

Lord, You know how easily our thoughts can wander, how they can get tangled in worries, distractions, and sometimes even lies. I pray that You would help each of us recognize when our minds are roaming and lead us back to the peace and security found in Your presence. Teach us to bring our thoughts under Your care and align them with Your truth.

In this sacred space of our subconscious, where so much is hidden, I ask that You help us clear away the clutter of doubt and confusion. Give us the courage to choose Your truth over the distractions that pull us away from You. May we find rest in knowing that our thoughts don't need to control us, but that You are our peace, our clarity, and our guide.

Thank You, Father, for being with us in this room of the mind, helping us transform it into a place of quiet strength and intentionality. I pray that each one of us would continue to grow in the ability to manage our thoughts, leaning on You as we walk forward in faith and trust.

In Jesus' Name, Amen

Closet

The Room of Shame and Surrender

> *"But when you pray, go away by yourself, shut the door behind you, and pray to your Father in private. Then your Father, who sees everything, will reward you."* —Matthew 6:6

In October 2011, I said "Yes" to something that I really, *really* wanted to say "No" to.

I was in a desperate spot. A few weeks before I'd been fired from a coaching position at a college without any warning. No bad review, no discussion of unfulfilled duties, no concerns about my conduct or anything. Just a summary dismissal.

It burned and I wanted to avoid the feeling again. In fact, I had decided that I was completely done with coaching as a career. So much of the job involves uncontrollable outcomes, and the stress had begun to wear away at me. Your destiny is literally in the hands of someone else, or a team of them. So I rewrote my resume and began applying to jobs outside the field.

But the Holy Spirit had something to say about this. In fact, I remember the exact moment I heard Him whisper, "Do it one more time."

I was reluctant. But when I hear the Holy Spirit speak, I try to quickly obey because I know that following and pursuing His leading will always take you to a place of safety. What I *didn't* know is that these safe places aren't physical, but spiritual, and that can be rather frightening.

I followed the call and found a coaching job that I thought for sure I wouldn't get. It was in the South, and I'd be the head coach of a men's team. As a Black woman, I couldn't imagine they'd see me as a good fit.

They hired me anyway, and I obediently accepted.

But I had my concerns, and it didn't take long for those concerns to become a problem.

The Other Candidate

While I was reluctant to coach again, accepting this new role felt like a fresh start. For the previous five years, I had led a women's only team, and I missed the competitiveness and grit of coaching young men. I cherished having a few people around who would commit to the process, and I found this more often when coaching men.

However, things quickly got weird.

During the interview process, the administration had mentioned an assistant coach they wanted me to keep on staff due to his strengths and past performance. I was open to this suggestion, mainly because the school year had already begun and it would be hard to find a replacement within the provided salary. Additionally, stability was crucial for the team as I learned the ropes.

What I didn't realize was that this assistant coach had also applied for the head coaching position—*my* position. In my first week on the job, he told me this. Then he added, "Yeah, they only hired you because you are a woman and you are Black."

I don't quite know what happened to my body in that moment, but I remember feeling numb and hotter than the sun. My face must have been a picture because I was aghast not only at his comment, but the brazenness of him even saying it.

It made no sense. I had actually been complimenting him and his work with the program, only for him to straight-up accuse me of being a DEI hire. I didn't respond, but just shook my head. I turned back to my computer as my teeth clenched in fury.

Then something happened: I buried it. I said nothing in return. I told no one in my life about it. I was ashamed because the man's boldness—his rigid resolve—told me that he genuinely believed what he'd said.

That belief, I now realize, was contagious.

So I stepped into the closet. Not a physical one, of course, but a mental and spiritual one. I went into hiding. I covered up my shame.

And I lived there for years.

I should have addressed the disrespect head-on. This should have been a write-up at the least, and honestly, I should have relieved him of his duties immediately.

But I didn't. Everything about that moment said, *No, you can't,* and I believed it.

This misstep haunted our working relationship for the next five years. It permeated the fabric of the team, although no one else really knew why there was a disconnect between us.

But I knew. Those words echoed in my mind for years.

They only hired you because you are a woman, and you are Black.

While it seems I have cause to hold that moment against him, the person I truly hold it against is myself.

That was the day I began questioning everything about my qualifications, abilities, talents, and skills. My resume spoke for itself, especially for a program in transition with low resources, which was a perfect fit for my strengths as an achiever, restorer, and self-assured leader.

Despite this, I couldn't escape my closet thinking. Every decision I made moving forward was tethered to those words.

I was stuck and had no idea how to get out.

The Closet of the Heart

If we're being honest, all of us have experienced something like this in our lives. We endured a traumatizing moment that made us feel shame, and despite feeling like we should push back, we don't.

This creates a double portion of shame: We've been wronged and know it, but don't have the courage or confidence to stand up for ourselves.

This leads to a life spent hiding in the "closet," a space normally reserved for storage, but often home to the things we hope no one finds out about us.

Today, closets are incredibly common. They serve as spaces for storing linens, household supplies, or clothing. But they actually have a rich history that tells the story of human innovation and societal evolution.

Some of the earliest adopters of closets were Roman soldiers who needed practical storage solutions for their weapons and armor during long journeys. These early storage units, known as "armoriums," eventually gave rise to the term "armoire."

Later, in the Middle Ages, when having a bedroom was a privilege reserved for the wealthy, most common folk slept in communal spaces like a great hall or a multi-purpose room that served as kitchen, living, and sleeping quarters. Bedrooms of the wealthy were multifunctional, used for sleeping, working, and entertaining guests, leaving little room for privacy.

Where could one hope to find a quiet place for solitude?

Enter the closet.

As the Medieval period drew to a close, affluent homeowners began adding closets adjacent to their bedrooms. These spaces were not locations to store treasured possessions but for retreats and sanctuaries for prayer, reading, and contemplation. The closet became the most private area in the home, a legacy that persists today as the word "closet" often connotes secrecy and privacy.

The concept of the closet as a built-in storage space took hold in the United States around 1840. Americans pioneered the idea of integrating closets directly into the walls of homes, making them a standard feature by the dawn of the 20th century. This innovation offered a convenient, cost-effective alternative to bulky furniture like armoires and chests. Ever since, closets have remained a functional but underappreciated part of the home.

Much like the closet's journey from a practical storage space to a symbol of privacy, our emotional and spiritual lives often mirror this progression.

The closet, in its original form, offered a hidden corner where we could retreat from the eyes of others; in much the same way, we sometimes use metaphorical "closets" to hide parts of ourselves from the world, whether it be pain, fear, guilt, or shame.

We stash away our deepest fears, our regrets, and our secrets, hoping no one will see them. And in this space, we can often feel isolated, hiding in the shadows of our own vulnerability.

But keeping this kind of shame locked away isn't healthy. It also isn't what God wants for us.

Paul provides a powerful baseline for this truth in Philippians: "Don't worry about anything; instead, pray about everything. Tell God what you need, and thank him for all he has done. Then you will experience God's peace, which exceeds anything we can understand. His peace will guard your hearts and minds as you live in Christ Jesus," (Philippians 4:6-7).

He continues, "Fix your thoughts on what is true, and honorable, and right, and pure, and lovely, and admirable. Think about things that are excellent and worthy of praise," (Philippians 4:8).

My relationship with the assistant coach was none of these things. The source of this isn't my fault; I'm not the one who brought shame into the picture, likely out of envy and spite.

But once my colleague sinned against me, the ball was entirely in my court to seek reconciliation. Yes, that would mean more uncomfortable conversations. It would possibly mean upsetting him, and my new employer. It could even convince my new community to judge me, thinking that I was a caricature or stereotype, and "angry Black woman" or some other trope.

Obeying the gospel takes courage. Protecting the closet of your heart—keeping it spacious so you can retreat there to pray, rather than hide or hoard—takes persistence and faith.

I'm grieved to say I didn't have those traits back then. I'm praying that I somehow have them now.

So instead of either reconciling or seeking justice, I capitulated and stuffed my pride in the closet. I avoided any actions or moments that might bring attention to my ethnicity and gender. I tip-toed around what I perceived to be his expectations and emotions. I bent over backwards to keep everyone happy.

Meanwhile, my heart-closet began to overflow with relics of shame and bitterness.

How I Escaped the "Closet"

Sometimes when we're trapped in cycles of bad thinking or poor decision-making, God sends one of His saints into our lives to provide the help we need.

That person—Terril—showed me how to escape the closet of shame and start living as God intended.

A phenomenal Black woman in the corporate world, Terril had faced immense challenges throughout her life, yet she refused to let those odds define her. She rose to become one of the most prominent Presidents/CEOs in her field, and when she spoke to me her words and presence resonated in a way I had never experienced from another woman.

Initially, I was taken aback by her directness and unwavering confidence. But I soon realized that her strength and determination weren't an attack; I only perceived them that way because they convicted me of my lack of confidence and surety!

Terril's words and character were exactly what I needed. Her relentless spirit began to chip away at the barriers I had built around myself. I realized I didn't just want to open the door of my closet; I wanted to rip it off its hinges and leap out, whether I was ready or not.

Her directness, and her ability to switch gears between personal and professional personas, taught me so much about resilience. She showed me that life is about balance and not letting a tough moment define your entire day or, in my case, an entire decade.

So to any woman reading this, hear me and the words Terril taught me: Embrace those challenging conversations, enjoy the unexpected moments, and always know you have the strength to grow and thrive through it all.

Without this woman's influence, I don't know if I would have ever found the courage to step out of my metaphorical closet and submit to God's renovating power. She fulfilled a deep spiritual need and led me to a turning point moment I will never forget.

We must come out of our spiritual closets. We must reject shame and its lies. We must discover what it means to have true courage, the kind of courage that stares down rejection and humiliation and says, "I'm not afraid."

And then we must trust God with our shame so we no longer need a place like a closet for shame. Only then can your closet be the place of prayer, praise and power that it was meant to be.

Resurrect Your Sanctuary

Just as the closet's history tells a story of moving from simple function to sacred space, we too can move beyond merely hiding our vulnerability to uncovering and allowing God to redeem those places in our hearts.

This process requires the courage to open the doors of our closets and invite God into those secret places we've long kept hidden. That means:

- Talking to trusted friends or professionals about moments of your life that cause you to feel shame

- Journaling and reflecting on those moments

- Praying without ceasing that you will have the courage to surrender these moments to the Lord, and that He will heal you from the trauma created by those moments

- Initiating difficult conversations with people who've wronged you, or whom you've wronged, in order to pursue reconciliation

- Spending more time in God's Word than in other sources of ideas—news, social media, TV and streaming—keeping the closet free of clutter

The closet's evolution reminds us that our vulnerability does not have to be a space of isolation and shame, but a sacred opportunity for healing and connection with God. It's in these quiet, hidden places that we have the chance to be most honest with ourselves and with God. The vulnerability that we might try to stuff away in the closet is actually the gateway to deeper intimacy with Him.

That's why surrender is at the core of escaping the closet and resurrecting it from death to life.

Managing shame requires the utmost control.

But surrender takes all of that and gives it to Jesus, proclaiming: "I trust you, even when it doesn't feel safe."

The world isn't safe. Relationships aren't safe. Even a successful job with a fat paycheck isn't safe.

The only true source of safety is in the intimate embrace of a loving God. But that can't happen when we're holding everything back from him. When we lock our hearts in the closet, terrified of what will happen when we're "found out," God can't perform his miraculous restorative work.

Beg for the courage to surrender. Ask for the Holy Spirit to give you faith in His resurrecting, renovating prowess.

Then begin taking steps, one at a time, to empty the closet and return it to its rightful place as a sanctuary.

No More Shame

When we confine the parts of ourselves that we think are shameful—our failures, passions, or perceived faults—we live out a lie. Everything we do is an attempt to present a curated, "clean" version of ourselves.

But that's not who we really are.

There's a lot I could say about what it means for me to be Black and a woman. Yet around my colleague, the male assistant coach, I did all I could to avoid being *his* perception of a Black woman. I changed everything. It wasn't all conscious, either. In fact, I stopped thinking about it soon after because I didn't want to be petty or overly emotional.

Yet in the closet of my heart, shame was doing its work, leaking out and poisoning every aspect of who I was and how I comported myself.

Worst of all, the shame we hide in the closet is a direct rejection of God's love for us.

God declares His love for His people in the words of the prophet Jeremiah: "I have loved you, my people, with an everlasting love. With unfailing love I have drawn you to myself," (Jeremiah 31:3).

And in Ephesians, Paul proclaims, "But God is so rich in mercy, and he loved us so much, that even though we were dead because of our sins, he gave us life when he raised Christ from the dead," (Ephesians 2:4-5).

Shame is the tool that Satan uses to pry us away from God. We are designed to be filled with His adoration, just as a baby isn't complete or whole without the love of its mother. God longs to make us complete in Him, and He does this by loving and sanctifying us.

That can't happen when we give shame a safe haven in our lives. We cannot truly enjoy His grace when we go on believing that grace can't apply to us.

For that is the nature of shame: A declaration that grace is dead for us. No wonder this is Satan's primary strategy!

This is why we must come out and purge our closets of the garbage living there. Shame has no place in the life of a Christ-follower. You are His, bought and paid for by the blood of Jesus Christ.

"For you know that God paid a ransom to save you from the empty life you inherited from your ancestors," Peter writes in his epistle. "And it was not paid with mere gold or silver, which lose their value. It was the precious blood of Christ, the sinless, spotless Lamb of God. God chose him as your ransom long before the world began, but now in these last days he has been revealed for your sake," (1 Peter 1:18–20).

Consider, dear one, the value of your soul to the Lord God Almighty. Weigh the cost of reconciling you for eternity.

And remember that God already knows every minute detail of your shame and He is not repulsed or deterred. He is not offended, mocked, or aghast at who you are. In fact, He gladly kneels to the ground and washes your feet, taking the place of a servant so that you can be exalted into the heavens.

It's time for shame to go.

And it's time to return to the closet with joy, anticipation, and peace, restoring it to a place of worship and rest.

In Christ, this is entirely possible.

I've found peace in the years since my conversation with the assistant coach. You, too, can bring anything imaginable to the father, surrender it, and enjoy remarkable freedom.

All you have to do is start the work.

Reflection Questions

1. What "closets" in your own life are you currently hiding in—metaphorical spaces where you stash away fears, regrets, or secrets out of shame?

2. Can you identify a specific traumatic moment that caused you to feel shame, where you knew you should push back but didn't? How has that moment impacted you since?

3. What specific actions can you take this week to begin emptying your "heart-closet" of shame and bitterness and returning it to a place of prayer and rest?

Journaling Prompt

What is one area of your life where you need to "beg for the courage to surrender" to God, even when it doesn't feel safe?

My Prayer for You

Father God,

Thank You for seeing the person reading this prayer—someone who has tucked away pieces of themselves, wondering if they'd ever be safe to bring into the light. You are the God who meets us in hidden places, who gently reveals truth in the dark, and who never stops pursuing us with love.

I lift them up to You now. You know the closets they've retreated to—spaces filled with shame, fear, confusion, or wounds too tender to name. I pray that You would lovingly call them out of hiding, reminding them that they are deeply known and unconditionally loved by You.

Break the grip of false identity, of imposter syndrome, and the pressure to perform. Quiet every voice that speaks lies, and let Your truth rise loud and clear. Remind them they were created with intention, beauty, and purpose.

Cover them in confidence—not the kind that boasts, but the kind rooted in knowing who they are in You. Teach them how to walk in vulnerability without fear, how to be open without shame. Let them step into freedom, no longer bound by who they were told to be, but walking fully in who You created them to become.

May they no longer shrink, hide, or carry the weight of masks. You are calling them out—and I pray they respond with a bold and surrendered yes.

In Jesus' Name, Amen

Basement

The Room of Foundations and Fractures

> *"If the foundations are destroyed, what can the righteous do?"* —Psalm 11:3

Sometimes people say things you wish they wouldn't. Sometimes these statements come out of nowhere and startle us with their severity. Occasionally these words are uncalled for, brash or overly critical.

But sometimes they flow directly from the mouth of God, which is precisely what happened to one of the Bible's greatest heroes.

King David is and was famous. The slayer of Goliath, the heir of the murderous King Saul, and the "man after God's own heart" who wrote dozens of psalms that we study today, David stands above most other characters in Christian history.

Yet he is the villain lurking at the center of a terrible event, a series of crimes that required a prophet of God to confront.

It happened to Israel's king thousands of years ago, and it happens today. Life seems to be going along fine, and suddenly there's a person calling you out.

This is what transpires when your foundation has begun to crack: Your anchor, the bedrock of your identity—the thing upon which all else rests.

The Basement.

This is the core of our being; it's also where the darkest, filthiest secrets slowly destroy the house upon which we've built our lives.

Cracks in the Kingdom

The story begins with David as King of Israel and the nation at war with the Ammonites. But unlike in the past, David was not leading his warriors into battle. He was home at his palace, enjoying the fruits of royalty.

Then one night, walking the roof, he looked down—likely through a window—and saw her: Bathsheeba, the wife of another man, bathing.

Scripture avoids any salacious details, simply declaring, "David sent messengers to get her; and when she came to the palace, he slept with her," (2 Samuel 11:4). Given the fact that she was married, and that David possessed immense power and prestige, it's more than likely he coerced her into this liaison.

Yet there's a twist. Soon after their intercourse, Bathsheeba sends the king a message: She's pregnant with *his* child. Horrified that his secret sin might be discovered, David immediately hatched a plot to have the husband returned from the front lines so that he might sleep with his wife and cover up the pregnancy.

But Uriah, the husband, refused. "The Ark and the armies of Israel and Judah are living in tents, and Joab and my master's men are camping in the open fields," the soldier told his king. "How could I go home to wine and dine and sleep with my wife? I swear that I would never do such a thing," (verse 11).

Foiled, David doubled down on the cover-up, but this time his plan was far more viscous. He sent Uriah to the front lines of the war with the Ammonites along with instructions to Joab, the commander: "Station Uriah on the front lines where the battle is fiercest. Then pull back so that he will be killed," (verse 15). Sure enough, the exposed soldier was slain in battle, along with several of his comrades.

"When Uriah's wife heard that her husband was dead, she mourned for him. When the period of mourning was over, David sent for her and brought her to the palace, and she became one of his wives. Then she gave birth to a son. But the Lord was displeased with what David had done," (2 Samuel 11:26–27).

With Bathsheeba's husband dead, David was confident that his secret was safe.

Yet the cracks in the Basement always announce their presence in the rudest ways, and at the most inopportune times.

Confronted and Convicted

It didn't take long for the Lord to react. And as He often does when those in power abuse their position, God sent a prophet, Nathan, to speak truth to the king.

Yet the Lord's message was clever. One might even call it a trap. For secret sin *always* evolves into a trap that catches us in our hypocrisy.

"There were two men in a certain town," Nathan said, telling King David a seemingly innocent story. "One was rich, and one was poor. The rich man owned a great many sheep and cattle. The poor man owned nothing but one little lamb he had bought. He raised that little lamb, and it grew up with his children. It ate from the man's own plate and drank from his cup. He cuddled it in his arms like a baby daughter. One day a guest arrived at the home of the rich man. But instead of killing an animal from his own flock or herd, he took the poor man's lamb and killed it and prepared it for his guest," (2 Samuel 12:1–4).

Immediately, the king was furious.

"As surely as the LORD lives," David vowed, "any man who would do such a thing deserves to die! He must repay four lambs to the poor man for the one he stole and for having no pity," (2 Samuel 12:5–6).

With these words, the trap sprang shut. The hypocrisy born of lust and greed and pride closed on the King of Israel like jaws closing on a bear.

"You are that man!" proclaimed Nathan, his voice likely a thunderous roar. "The Lord, the God of Israel, says: I anointed you king of Israel and saved you from the power of Saul. I gave you your master's house and his wives and the kingdoms of Israel and Judah. And if that had not been enough, I would have given you much, much more. Why, then, have you despised the word of the Lord and done this horrible deed? For you have murdered Uriah the Hittite with the sword of the Ammonites and stolen his wife. From this time on, your family will live by the sword because you have despised me by taking Uriah's wife to be your own."

Even after this prophetic curse—that David's family line would be stained by constant betrayal, in-fighting, and bloodshed—Nathan wasn't finished.

"This is what the LORD says," he continued. "Because of what you have done, I will cause your own household to rebel against you. I will give your wives to another man before your very eyes, and he will go to bed with them in public view. You did it secretly, but I will make this happen to you openly in the sight of all Israel," (2 Samuel 12:7–12).

Listening to story, I pray that I never ensnare myself so deeply that a prophet has to come and condemn my family like this!

Yet without Nathan's words, David and the entire nation of Israel would have been caught in an even more dangerous trap—that of generational evil.

David's power had clearly gone to his head. Instead of leading soldiers in war, he was relaxing on his roof and peeping at bathing women. He used that power to coerce another man's wife into sex, bribe Uriah, and eventually order Uriah's death—all with seeming impunity. No one in David's inner circle questioned him or his actions. It required the literal messenger of God to bring David's sin to his attention.

While David had once been a shining example of obedience, he had fallen into addiction and entitlement. He had lost the essence of what it meant to be God's beloved.

His foundation was splintering like a lightning bolt.

So it is with us: We move from a season of faith and compliance into another of rebellion or manipulation. We keep things hidden; we tell little lies that balloon into grander lies.

Then the whole house of our lives violently shifts to the side, all because of the erosion happening in the depths.

This is the fearsome danger of secret sin.

And this is why God is so adamant that we root it out and repair it with His gospel truth.

The Dark Place

When people think of basements today, they often imagine game rooms, home theaters, or cozy guest suites. Pinterest boards are filled with pictures of beautifully renovated spaces, complete with plush carpet and recessed lighting. But that was never the basement's original intent.

Originally, the basement was built for function, not flair. It was the lowliest part of the house—partially or completely underground—intended to hold what was necessary but not pretty. It was dark, damp, and out of sight. This is where you put things you didn't want to see or let others see; it was a storage area for things you didn't know what to do with, or didn't have the heart to throw away. Old photographs. Broken appliances. Dusty boxes of forgotten memories. Heirlooms too sentimental to display and too painful to revisit. This was not a room for company; this was a room for containment.

The basement often contains vital components of a house's infrastructure. The water heater or furnace; pipes, ducts, and wiring. Some homes even hide the breaker box in the basement, forcing you to brave the cobweb-infested darkness to restore power when a switch goes off.

In addition, the basement holds something even more important: The *foundation*. This is the literal support structure for the rest of the house, holding up everything that rises above.

No matter how beautiful the living room looks, how modern the kitchen is, or how peaceful the bedroom feels, if the basement's foundation is cracked or unstable, everything above it is at risk.

Spiritually, the basement is symbolic of the hidden places in our lives—the things we've tucked away, buried, or sealed off. It's the private storage room of our soul, filled with stories and scars, secrets and struggles. It's where we put the things that aren't "Sunday best," topics we don't talk about at Bible study or post about on social media.

Yet what's hidden in the Basement has the power to shape everything above it.

Some of us have avoided this space for years. We've remodeled every other room in our spiritual house, hoping that if the surface looked good enough, no one would notice the cracks underneath.

But the truth is, people *do* notice. Just like in a physical home, the signs of foundation issues eventually make their way upstairs—crooked doors, sagging floors, and shifting walls.

Sooner or later, what's buried finds its way to the surface.

Of course, we all keep secrets. Some are harmless and somewhat embarrassing, like the story of a first kiss or the truth that you bit your toenails as a kid. Others are vicious and ripe with humiliation: Truths of betrayal; shameful mistakes and sins; hidden beliefs or motives that we dare not bring out of the dark and into the light.

Every secret is something more: It's a core belief.

What you keep hidden away reveals a lot about you.

Not willing to tell your spouse about previous relationships? That's a belief about your relationship, yourself, and the possibility of being forgiven.

Not ready to share your questions about God? That's a belief that doubt or inquisitiveness is a sin in itself, and therefore unforgivable.

Beliefs are the foundation of who we are. They undergird everything we say, think, and do. They also shape our plans for the future and our feelings about them, whether optimistic or cynical.

That's why when we keep them secret, they're so dangerous: They're the silent, invisible puppetmasters pulling the strings of our character.

Why Basement Cracks Are So Dangerous

Let's talk about cracks.

Not just the kind you see in sidewalks or driveways, but the kind that show up in the foundation of your life, cracks that are usually invisible until the pressure builds or the storms hit.

You know the ones I mean—the compromises we make, the truths we suppress, the wounds we bury so deep that even we forget they're there. That is, until something shifts, and suddenly we're face to face with them.

What's wild is that other people can often see the signs before we do. Just like a house showing signs of foundation issues, our lives begin revealing these faults, a little at a time: A short temper; withdrawn behavior; unhealthy patterns we keep repeating.

But here's the kicker: Most of us are so used to the tilt of our own houses that we don't realize how off-center things have become.

In my own life, I've had moments where someone would gently—or not so gently—ask, "Are you okay?" And deep down, I knew they weren't asking about my schedule or my mood—they were asking about my basement. The stuff I kept hidden. The stuff I had convinced myself didn't matter anymore.

And here's the truth: These cracks won't fix themselves, and ignoring them only makes them worse. Paul alludes to this truth when he writes, "Be not deceived: God is not mocked, for whatever one sows, that will he also reap," (Galatians 6:7-8).

Anyone who has done foundation work on a house knows that it isn't easy, quick, or cheap. Such work takes a significant investment.

But who would argue that it's worth it, if the entire house is at stake?

How much more is your life at stake when the truth of a shattered foundation begins to reveal itself?

When the secrets and beliefs stashed in our Basements become apparent, it is imperative that we attack the problem with a fiery passion. The risk of inaction is simply too great.

The Rock and the Sand

A foundation is only as good as the structure beneath it. Jesus's First Century audience knew as much, and that's why Jesus used the idea of home construction as a core metaphor about following His teachings:

"'Anyone who listens to my teaching and follows it is wise, like a person who builds a house on solid rock," Jesus says at the conclusion of the Sermon on the Mount. "Though the rain comes in torrents and the floodwaters rise and the winds beat against that house, it won't collapse because it is built on bedrock. But anyone who hears my teaching and doesn't obey it is foolish, like a person who builds a house on sand. When the rains and floods come and the winds beat against that house, it will collapse with a mighty crash,'" (Matthew 7:24-27).

Every autumn, hurricanes hit the southern Atlantic coast, pushing water over the sandy beaches. And inevitably, news cameras capture startling images of expensive beach homes collapsing into the sea.

It's as if Jesus could see the future....

Clearly not all foundations are built on the same stuff. It's also clear that there's something sacred about knowing your foundation, and the substance under it, is strong.

But this requires regular inspection and maintenance, confession and repentance. It's not just a one-time construction job. It's an ongoing process.

When I think about the seasons I neglected my foundation, it was never because I didn't care. It was because I thought I didn't have time, or worse, that I could ignore the flaws and keep them hidden in perpetuity.

But here's the thing about foundations: What you build on top of them will always reflect what's underneath.

When Someone Walks Into Your Basement

When Nathan told David the story of the rich man and poor man, he was pointing out the rampant damage to the king's foundation.

The last thing you or I want is someone walking into our Basements. After all, that's where all the secrets are hidden.

Yet I'm reminded of this passage from James: "Confess your sins to one another and pray for one another, that you may be healed," (James 5:16).

That's the thing about divine appointments. God doesn't send people to condemn you; He sends people to confront you in love, to help you excavate what's been buried so you can rebuild better.

And just like the prophet Nathan, sometimes the people God uses are bold enough to say what no one else will. You better believe that kind of truth is hard to hear. But the spiritual weight of it will be impossible to ignore.

Even Nathan's words to David weren't about shame—they were full of grace. How evil would it be to let David live in ignorance of his wicked sin! To go on lusting, murdering, and stealing other men's wives!

But because God is jealous for our love and committed to the blessings of walking with Him, God reached out through Nathan. He creates ways to break through our defenses and say, "I see you. I love you. And I want better for you." He did this with King David, and He'll do it with you.

Restoring a Damaged Foundation

Starting the work of restoring our foundation is never easy, primarily because we rarely notice the problems until disaster strikes. A relationship ends, the job falls through, the diagnosis comes, or life just knocks the wind out of you. And suddenly, what you thought was solid starts shifting under your feet.

That's when you realize: *This house needs work.*

I remember talking to a contractor who said, "Cracks aren't the problem—they're evidence of a problem."

Whew. That'll preach.

Some of us are walking around with foundational cracks that haven't been dealt with for years—maybe even decades. We've just figured out how to decorate *around* them. We redefine them as "character" or "charm."

But cracks are what they are: Evidence of worsening damage.

Just like in a real house, no amount of cute paint or trendy furniture can cover structural damage.

Of course, foundations can be repaired. But it requires honesty, dedication, and considerable investment.

Most of all, it means that you have to *go down there*, shine a light, and assess the damage. And you probably won't leave for quite a long time.

Spiritually, that's where **confession** and **repentance** come in. I'm not just talking about listing out your wrongs like a checklist. I mean admitting the 'why' behind the what. Digging into the ugly truth of the heart. Refusing to defend or explain, but to simply reveal.

That's the beginning of healing.

The Apostle John declares, "If we confess our sins, he is faithful and just to forgive us our sins and to cleanse us from all unrighteousness," (1 John 1:9). This is one of the greatest promises in all Scripture: If we trust His process, we can enjoy complete forgiveness and redemption.

Don't miss that. God's way isn't punishment. It's restoration.

Keep in mind that God isn't afraid of your basement because He already knows what's down there. He's just waiting for your surrender so He can start the demo and rebuild.

Let Him Rebuild Your Foundation

If you've been avoiding your own Basement—whether out of fear, shame, or just sheer exhaustion—know this: You're not alone.

Every woman I've ever sat with has a basement story. Society and its overseer, Satan, convince us to feel shame about a million different things, most of which we hide in the dark shadows of our subconscious. Men are subject to this too, and my beloved husband has offered his fair share of stories about God's work in *his* Basement.

But sadly, many people refuse to invite God into the Basement. Few are willing to let Him do His work to turn it into a testimony.

Remember the words of Jesus: "Anyone who hears my teaching and doesn't obey it is foolish, like a person who builds a house on sand. When the rains and floods come and the winds beat against that house, it will collapse with a mighty crash," (Matthew 7:26-27).

Let me say it like I would if we were sitting across from each other on the couch, sipping a tasty beverage:

Two builders had houses. They both went through storms. The difference wasn't what their houses *looked* like. It was what they were *standing on*.

And let's be honest: The foundation is the part nobody claps for. No one's jaw drops when they see an upgraded or repaired foundation. Nobody's out here admiring your crawl space or concrete slab.

But that's the part that matters when life hits, when betrayal stings, when the finances dry up, and when the prayer you prayed doesn't get answered the way you hoped.

That's when the foundation shows itself. That's when you find out whether your life is built on His Word or your feelings, on truth or convenience, on rock or sand.

And I get it—building on the rock takes longer. It's not flashy. It's not fun.

But it holds.

Jesus didn't say *if* the rain comes—He said *when*. The storm is part of the story.

But the outcome? That depends on the foundation.

So again I ask you, from one friend to another: What is your house *really* built on?

I'm not just talking about your Sunday answers. I'm talking about the real stuff. The quiet choices. The motives nobody sees. The conversations you have in your mind when you're lonely, tired, or running low on confidence.

Is your foundation really God's Word and presence?

Or is it your hustle? Your trauma? Your charm?

The basement is where you find out.

And if today you're realizing that you've been building on something unstable, that's not shame talking—that's grace. That's the Spirit of God saying, "Let's go back to the foundation. Let's rebuild—this time with Me at the center."

You're not disqualified. You're not too far gone. And you're not alone.

That's what the prophet Nathan said to David when he had to confront him. It was not his wish to destroy David, but to redeem him.

Sometimes God sends a Nathan into our lives. Sometimes you *are* the Nathan. Either way, it's always about restoration.

So, let's get low. Let's get real. Let's get to the basement.

Because that's where the real beauty is found.

Reflection Questions

1. What are some things in your own "basement" that you've kept hidden from others, and how have they affected your life, even if they've been buried for a long time?

2. Have you experienced a moment when a "crack" in your spiritual or emotional foundation became evident? How did you respond, and what did you learn from that experience?

3. How can forgiveness—both toward others and ourselves—be a key to healing the secrets in our spiritual "basement"?

Journaling Prompt

Reflecting on the metaphor of a "basement," what would it look like for you to begin rebuilding or strengthening the spiritual foundation of your life?

My Prayer for You

Father God,

 Thank you for the grace and love You extend to us, even in the deepest, darkest parts of our lives. I lift up every person reading this, and I ask that You would gently guide her to the hidden spaces in her soul—the places she's tried to forget or keep locked away. Father, You know what lies beneath the surface, and You know the weight that can come from carrying secrets and unresolved pain.

 Lord, shine Your light into her spiritual basement and bring healing to those areas that may have been ignored or forgotten. May Your love be the light that pierces through the darkness, offering grace where there has been shame, comfort where there has been fear, and restoration where there has been brokenness. Help her to trust that You are not asking her to face these secrets alone. You are with her, and You are already rebuilding her foundation. Give her the courage to face what has been buried for too long, to confess what needs to be confessed, and to forgive what needs to be forgiven.

 Lord, I ask for strength and wisdom as she begins the work of healing and restoration. May she feel the support of Your Holy Spirit as You walk with her, step by step, through the process of spiritual renewal. May she experience the beauty of a life built on the solid rock of Your Word, a foundation that will not waver when the storms come. Thank You for Your unfailing love, Your patience, and Your desire for us to live fully in the freedom You provide. May her foundation be firm, her heart healed, and her spirit renewed.

 In Jesus' Name, Amen

THE HEART

THE HOME OF FAITH AND FREEDOM

> "In him the whole building is joined together and rises to become a holy temple in the Lord. And in him you too are being built together to become a dwelling in which God lives by his Spirit." — Ephesians 2:21-22 (NIV)

You've walked through every room of your heart, noticing quiet corners, spaces that spark warmth, and those that carry shadows or echoes of old fears. Some rooms may have felt familiar and safe, places where you could breathe and simply be. Others may have challenged you, stirred up old wounds, or invited you to face truths you hadn't wanted to see.

Wherever you are in this journey, know this:

Every room matters, every story matters, and every corner of your heart is seen and known by God.

"Do you not know that you are God's temple and that His Spirit dwells in you?" (1 Corinthians 3:16)

This isn't about making each room perfect. Perfect is a lie. It's about inviting the beautiful presence of the Lord Jesus into every room of your heart and allowing His Spirit to remake it in His image.

Take a moment to pause. Inhale. Let yourself feel the fullness of the journey you've walked so far.

As you stand at the threshold of your heart, take a moment to consider this: What fills your inner rooms does not stay hidden. As the Scriptures remind us, "Out of the abundance of the heart the mouth speaks," (Matthew 12:34). The stories, fears, and joys you carry shape the words you speak — to yourself, to others, and to God.

The Heart as Home

More than ever, you can appreciate how your heart is its own spiritual house. And that house is composed of individual rooms, each of which tells its own story. Every room has a part to play in your story, adding to the whole of your Self.

In the Living Room, perhaps you've experienced silence that felt heavy, or words you longed to speak but couldn't. Maybe you've carried unspoken truths, wondering if anyone would understand. These quiet spaces can shape how you connect with others, but they can also become doors to courage — doors waiting for you to step through and speak your truth. You might consider journaling or praying about what you've been holding back. Ask God to guide you in discernment: *Is it time to speak? Is it time to pray?*

Every room of your heart matters, because "out of the heart flows the issues of life," (Proverbs 4:23). The fears, joys, regrets, and love you nurture inside will influence the paths you walk, the conversations you have, and the way you interact with those you love."

In the Kid's Room, maybe you've ever felt like you weren't quite enough, or like you were missing the "red bag" that would let you belong. Perhaps opportunities or relationships seemed just out of reach because you doubted yourself or waited for someone else's validation. Remember that belonging often begins with *seeing yourself as God sees you*. You can start small: a prayer of gratitude, a reflection on your gifts, or an affirmation of your worth in His eyes.

In the Closet, perhaps you've hidden moments of shame, regret, or fear. Maybe someone wronged you, or circumstances made you doubt your worth, and instead of addressing it, you tucked it away. These Closets are common to us all. They remind us that what is hidden doesn't have to define us, and that surrender — not suppression — creates space for God's healing. You might consider gently bringing these moments to God in prayer, asking for His perspective and for the courage to forgive yourself or others when the time is right.

Even in the Basement, where fractures and hidden struggles lie, God can meet you. Perhaps there are patterns in your life that need reflection, reconciliation, or release.

You don't have to fix everything today. Sometimes the first step is simply noticing, acknowledging, and offering it up to God.

Living in Your House

Your journey doesn't end with this book. Just as a home requires care, your heart needs tending. The workbook accompanying this book is a tool to help you:

- Revisit rooms that need attention or healing.

- Reflect on patterns that shape your choices, words, and relationships.

- Pray, journal, and map steps toward courage, restoration, and growth.

Some rooms may call to you more urgently than others. Some may surprise you with what you discover. That's okay.

Faith and freedom are companions, not destinations — they are present in every season, in every room, in every moment.

Gentle Invitations for Your Heart

- Are there words you've wanted to say but have been afraid to share?
- Is there forgiveness you've been holding back — for yourself, someone else, or even a child?
- Is there a memory or relationship you've tucked away that longs for acknowledgment or prayer?
- What small step could you take today to honor your heart without feeling pressured or unsafe?

You don't have to do everything at once. Begin where you are. God can meet you in quiet reflection, in private prayer, or in the first safe step toward reconciliation or healing.

It's time to step back into your life with intention, courage, and grace. Your journey isn't over — it's only beginning.

Keep the doors open. Invite God in.

And let Him renovate your heart into something more beautiful than you can possibly imagine.

My Heart's Blessing to You

May your Living Room echo with truth and grace, a space where silence is safe but words are powerful.

May your Kitchen overflow with courage and creativity, and may risk become a doorway, not a barrier.

May your Kid's Room remind you that you belong, that your story matters, and that adventure awaits when God invites you forward.

May your Bedrooms hold warmth, intimacy, and vulnerability without fear.

May your Bathroom always be a place of refreshment and release, where tears are sacred and healing begins.

May your Office guide your obligations with wisdom, discernment, and integrity.

May your Closet be a place of surrender, where shame is released and God's freedom fills the space.

May your Basement hold a foundation so strong that even storms cannot shake it.

And above all, may your heart—your earthly home—be the dwelling place of faith and freedom, a sacred space where God meets you in every room, restores you fully, and invites you to live boldly and freely.

In Jesus' Name,
Amen

About the Author

Natalie Smith-Wells is a dynamic Bible teacher, transformative coach, facilitator, and speaker known for her transparency, humor, and unfiltered passion for applying God's Word to everyday life. With nearly two decades of experience coaching and empowering women, Natalie has run alongside hundreds of women, championing the underdog and guiding them toward clarity, courage, and wholeness.

Her debut book, *Renovating the Heart*, along with its companion workbook, blends personal testimony with biblical truth to invite readers into a deep and honest exploration of the "rooms" of their spiritual house. Through her writing, Natalie helps women welcome God into the places where healing, renovation, and renewal are most needed.

Natalie continues to teach, speak, and create transformative spaces where women grow spiritually and walk in purpose with uncompromising integrity. She resides in Texas with her husband, Rodney.

BEGIN YOUR RENOVATION

Renovating the heart is never easy. Just like a typical household "flip," the hard work of renovation takes time, patience, determination, and relentless faith.

For those who are ready to take up the challenge, don't miss the 10-Session Companion Study Guide for *Renovating the Heart: Inviting God to Cleanse, Renew, and Redeem Every Room of Your Spiritual House.*

Scan the QR code to learn more and get your copy today!

www.ingramcontent.com/pod-product-compliance
Lightning Source LLC
LaVergne TN
LVHW090027080426
835812LV00043B/787